marques vickers

TWISTED TOUR GUIDE TO PITTSBURGH

SHOCKING DEATHS, SCANDALS AND VICE

By Marques Vickers

MARQUIS PUBLISHING
TACOMA, WASHINGTON

Copyright @2022 Marques Vickers

Version 1.1

Published by Marquis Publishing
Tacoma, Washington
TwistedTourGuides.com

Vickers, Marques, 1957

TWISTED TOUR GUIDE TO PITTSBURGH
Shocking Deaths, Scandals and Vice

Dedication: To my daughters Charline and Caroline. Thanks Mary For Riding Shotgun During Photography.

TABLE OF CONTENTS

SOURCES AND ARCHIVES SOURCED

PittsburghMagazine.com, Pittsburgh Post-Gazette, Wikipedia.org, Sites.rootsweb.com, WritersofWrongs.com, *Pittsburg: The Dark Years* by Steve Mellon, Facebook.com, Los Angeles Herald, WPXI.com, Triblive.com, Pghcitypaper.com, Timesonline.com, InsideEdition.com, Heavy.com, Pulse.Chatham.edu, CarnegieLibrary.org, Lebomag.com, PittsburghBeautiful.com, Playhouse.Pointpark.edu, Local-Pittsburgh.com, WTAE.com, ThePittsburghHistoryJournal.com, Baaa-Acre.com, Scholarship.law.upenn.edu, Los Angeles Times, New York Times, Washington Post, HistoricalDilettante.Blogspot.com, CinemaTreasures.org, Law.resource.org, TheDailyBeast.com, NYFA.edu, Post-Gazette.com, TheMagazineAntiques.com, History.com, Legacy.com, TampaBayTribune.com, GangsterReport.com, TubeCityOnline.com, Law.Justia.com, Northwestgeorgianews.com, ExplorePaHistory.com, Lawrencevillehistoricalsociety.com, Media.Defense.gov, ArlingtonCemetery.net, Airfields-Freeman.com, NFPA.org , HistoricalCrimeDetective.com, HauntedPittsburghTours.com, BrooklineConnection.com, HeinzHistoryCenter.org, Aviation-Safety.net, USDeadlyEvents.com, Skeptics.StackExchange.com, FireEngineering.com, Pittsburgh.CBSLocal.com, HauntsandHistory.blogspot.com, EConnection.com, DigitalArchives.PowerLibrary.org, The Wheeling Intelligencer, PopularPittsburgh.com, Jstor.org, Omnihotel.com, Pittsburgh Press, Broadwayworld.com, Inmatelocator.cor.pa.gov, Oxygen.com Pittsburgh.CBSlocal.com, SimonSculpture.com, WESA.fm, Law.Justia.com, Sun-Sentinel.com, MontourHeightsCC.com, and Telegram.com.

Photography shot during 2022. Some of the locations may have altered with time and ownership changes. Many of the locations are still privately inhabited. Please don't disturb the residents.

TWISTED TOUR GUIDE TO SAN DIEGO

Avoid The Tourist Herds.

What could be more uninspiring than seeing the identical attractions that everyone else has for decades?

This Twisted Tour Guide escorts you to the places locals don't want to talk about anymore…the same places people once couldn't stop talking about. Long after the screaming headlines and sensationalism has subsided, these bizarre, infamous and obscure historical sites remain hidden awaiting rediscovery.

Each visitation site in this guide is accompanied by a story. Many of the narratives defy believability, yet they are true. The profiled cast of characters feature saints and sinners (with emphasis towards the latter).

Notorious crimes, murders, accidental deaths, suicides, kidnappings, vice and scandal are captivating human interest tales. Paranormal activity in the aftermath is common.

The photography from each profile showcases the precise location where each event occurred. The scenes can seem ordinary, weird and sometimes very revealing towards clarifying the background behind events.

If you're seeking an alternative to conventional tourism, this Twisted Tourist Guide is ideal. Each directory accommodates the restless traveler and even resident looking for something unique and different. You will never imagine or scrutinize the Pittsburgh region through rose tinted glasses again.

George Washington's Seven Visits To Pittsburgh

**Washington Crossing Bridge (40th Street Bridge),
Pittsburgh
Herrs Island, Pittsburgh**

George Washington lived a fabled life documented as both action oriented and myth. During his initial encounter with Pittsburgh in 1753, he barely survived the raging Allegheny River. He and explorer Christopher Gist had set out to visit the current Point Park along with two French outposts at Venango and Fort LeBoeuf near Lake Eire.

The 21-year-old colonial major's mission was to survey and act as a diplomatic messenger for the British government. The French were not intimidated by his appearance. He arrived into the region during inclement November and returned to worsening conditions during late December.

Their horses were in poor condition so the pair set off on foot attempting to cross the Allegheny River on a crude raft. The raft couldn't withstand the rapids, overturned and the men were tossed into the icy waters. They barely survived swimming ashore at one of two speculated locations. These locations were either the still existing Herrs Island or the now sunken Wainwright Island near the Lawrenceville shoreline.

When they finally reported to Lt. General Robert Dinwiddle of Virginia, he honored their travels with a pamphlet detailing their journey favorably. It was widely circulated and read. Painter Carl Rakeman would later commemorate their exploit with a 19th century painting entitled *Washington Crossing the Allegheny*.

Washington's next three visits to the Pittsburgh region were of a military nature. In 1754, he returned with a troop of English soldiers that were soundly defeated by the French.

The next year, he accompanied General Edward Braddock with colonial troops en route to Fort Duquesne at the Point. They were surprise attacked and soundly beaten by the French in the *Battle of Monongahela.*

His fourth trip came with General John Forbes and British soldiers. They built a road across Pennsylvania during 1758. Their force secured a victory without firing a shot. The outnumbered French fled from Fort Duquesne before their arrival.

His fifth trip came in 1770 when he arrived to inspect real estate that he'd purchased in what is now Perryopolis. He stopped for a visit at Fort Pitt and took a canoe ride down the Ohio River.

His sixth trip in 1784 involved doing research for Virginia Governor Thomas Jefferson. He investigated whether linking a canal from the Potomac River to the Ohio River was feasible.

His final visit came in the capacity as President when he led a force of 12,000 American soldiers to quell the remnants of the Whiskey Rebellion. It would become the sole example when a sitting American president would lead troops into potential battle.

The Washington Crossing Bridge, commonly known as the 40th Street Bridge was opened in 1924 accommodating three lanes of traffic. The span crossing the Allegheny River received its name due its geographical proximity to the sunken island where Washington and Gist spent a freezing December night after their raft overturned. An additional Washington sculptural monument is located in Allegheny Commons Park on the North Side.

Capital Punishment on the Western Frontier
Firstside Park *(Former Boyd's Hill):*
Corner Grant and First Avenue, Pittsburgh

A decade following the conclusion of the Revolutionary War, Thomas Dunning was a private stationed at Fort Fayette under the command of General Anthony Wayne. The garrison succeeded the former Fort Pitt and current Point Park.

His rifle company was under great duress and pressure in preparation for battle with Native American tribes along the western frontier. Their prior skirmishes had languished under the command of Generals Harmar and St. Clair.

In a drunken rage, Dunning stabbed his wife Catherine Worthington to death on July 30, 1792. Suffering immediate remorse, he attempted suicide with the same weapon. Relations between the couple were reportedly *good* prompting no previous malice behind the attack.

Absent of court-appointed therapists or psychological profiles, his legal options were limited. He confessed to the crime. He was convicted of murder on September 5, 1792 and sentenced to death by hanging. Three months later Pennsylvania's first Governor Thomas Mifflin rejected his pardon request. Leading up to his execution, Dunning *displayed the strongest symptoms of sorrow and distress and every appearance of contrition and repentance.*

His repentant disposition mattered little.

On Saturday, January 26, 1793, Dunning would be escorted to the gallows on Boyd's Hill and hung. He earned the distinction of being Allegheny County's first civil execution. Later newspaper accounts itemized the financial expenses associated with his punishment.

Boyd's Hill would ultimately become flattened and over two centuries later, has become a parkland area.

General Anthony Wayne would prevail against hostile Native American forces in August 1794 in the *Battle of Fallen Timbers*. The result altered Pittsburgh's status from becoming simply a frontier boundary. The expanding settlement was now a thoroughfare for the hastening westward migration.

**The Whiskey Rebellion and George Washington Leading
The Enforcement
Bower Hill Historical Marker
310 Kane Boulevard, Pittsburgh**

Following the American Revolution, the expense of securing independence from Great Britain proved steep for individual states. The mounting debts incurred with few means of incoming revenue stimulated creative thinking for raising funds.

In 1790, Treasury Secretary Alexander Hamilton lobbied for the federal government to assume these debts. One of his solutions was to access an excise tax on whiskey. President George Washington initially opposed the idea, but traveled throughout Virginia and Pennsylvania to listen to his constituents' opinions regarding the proposal.

Washington met primarily with local government officials who welcomed the tax to ease their burden. It was unclear how many small farmers, producers and taxpayers he encountered. Washington returned with an assurance of local support and Congress passed the tax bill.

Washington's confidence for compliance proved erroneous. Protests against the passage became immediate amongst smaller enterprises. Large producers were given hefty tax incentives to produce more. Smaller producers paid a disproportionate level of tax based on their lesser yields.

Since only cash was accepted for payment, small producers simply refused to pay. They aggressively intimidated tax officials hired to collect.

Western Pennsylvania became a flashpoint for violence. On September 11, 1791, eleven men dressed as women surrounded excise officer Robert Johnson. He was stripped naked, tarred and feathered and his horse was stolen. He was left abandoned in a nearby forest.

Johnson recognized two of his assailants and follow-up arrest warrants were issued. A Cattle driver named John Connor was sent to arrest the men. He was attacked, tied to a tree and left in the forest for five hours. Realizing that tax enforcement offered detrimental prospects towards his health, Connor resigned.

Over the next few years, incidents escalated and the home of Pennsylvania excise officer Benjamin Wells was ransacked twice during 1793. His wife and children were menaced. During the second break-in, six disguised men demanded Wells to turn over his account books at gunpoint. They vehemently encouraged his immediate resignation.

The region became aflame with succession sentiments away from the federal government. More moderate members urged conciliatory measures.

On July 14, 1794, federal marshal David Lenox made a fateful decision to serve writs to 60 distillers who'd refused to pay the tax. The following day, Lenox and his guide, wealthy landowner John Neville began serving these delinquent accounts.

The pair approached the home of William Miller. Miller refused the summons. Following an intense argument, Lennox and Neville rode off…but not far. They encountered an unruly mob, fortified by liquor, pitchforks and loaded muskets.

The mob eventually allowed the two men to pass. A warning shot was fired in their direction. Rather than signaling an end to the hostilities, the conflict was igniting.

A larger gang of boisterous men awakened John Neville the next morning inside his home on Bower Hill. Some of this contingent had been served summons the previous day. They were in no mood for compromise. They insisted that Neville join them because there had been *a threat to his life*. He refused understanding their intention and ordered them off his property. To illustrate his point, he snatched a gun from inside and shot in their direction. He struck and killed Oliver Miller.

The mob responded by firing towards his house. Neville barely escaped. He summoned his slaves to arms with a signal horn. His group fired repeatedly into the crowd wounding six. The crowd retreated carrying Miller's body and their wounded. Neville was certain of their return.

The following day, 700 raggedy men assembled and marched to drum patter towards Neville's house. Ten soldiers had been commissioned the previous evening to protect Neville and his property. Their commanding officer assisted in enabling his escape.

Hopelessly outnumbered, the soldiers steadfastly refused to surrender. The mob ignored them. They torched the barn and slave dwellings. After allowing the Neville women to flee to safety, they opened gunfire on the main residence. The hour-long fusillade resulted in mob leader James McFarlane being shot to death. Enraged by his death, the attackers set the house on fire. The soldiers expediently surrendered without consequence.

The Bower Hill estate became a scattering of charred ashes.

Following their perceived success, the mob contemplated escalating an assault on Pittsburgh. Fearing extensive violence, a city delegation negotiated a truce. The agreement was solemnized by several gifted barrels of whiskey. The liquor placated the unfocused fury. Mob participants streamed peacefully through Pittsburgh.

The repercussions from the destruction of Bower Hill reverberated throughout Washington D.C. Alexander Hamilton wanted to send troops immediately. Washington preferred a peace envoy. The envoy approach failed. Washington then assembled a militia of 12,000 men from surrounding states to march into Western Pennsylvania.

Washington met with rebel leaders. They assured him that his militia was unnecessary. Washington sent the troops anyway anxious to quell any movements towards rebellion. They were greeted with disdain by locals, but no accompanying violence. The original instigators had already fled. Suspected participants were arrested and transferred to Philadelphia to stand trial. Two were found guilty of treason. Washington pardoned both men.

The proactive federal response proved an important precedent in establishing the credibility of federal authority. The whiskey tax remained intact until 1802. President Thomas Jefferson repealed it. The pragmatic Jefferson recognized the tax's unpopularity and ultimate impossibility to collect.

Pittsburgh Final Duel Over Idealism and Honor
Craft Park Dueling Site:
Craft Place at Craft Avenue and Boulevard of the Allies,
Pittsburgh

Modern political discourse appears benignly subdued when compared with the consequences of disagreement over two centuries ago. Today's flaming rhetoric may provoke a greater numbers reach via faceless legions on social media. The rhetoric rarely manifests into physical violence. During the eighteenth and early nineteenth century, men often fought to the death over ideals.

Pittsburgh's final acknowledged duel was staged at Craft Park with fatal consequences for one of the combatants. The locale then was on the periphery of town distant from curious spectators.

Tarleton Bates was born on May 22, 1775. He was one of twelve children of Quaker Thomas Bates from Virginia. At 18, Tarleton relocated to Pittsburgh and obtained employment with the Federal Quartermaster's Department. In 1800, he was appointed a protonotary of Allegheny County, a prestigious law clerk position.

He was considered *delicate*, *gentle* and *sensitive*. He developed an attachment to Emily Morgan, but the couple would never marry. He cultivated numerous political and social friendships that furthered his obsession with local politics.

In 1805, Bates and two friends Walter Forward and Henry Baldwin became publishers of a local Democratic Party newspaper called *The Tree of Liberty*. All three were young, upwardly ambitious and outspoken in their beliefs. Two would compile impressive professional careers.

Walter Forward would become a member of Congress and Treasury secretary under President John Tyler. Henry Baldwin would also serve in Congress and later become a Supreme Court justice.

The trio's opposition paper, *The Commonwealth* sparred relentlessly with them in print. Their 20-year-old publisher, Ephraim Pentland had arrived into Pittsburgh from Philadelphia.

A particularly contentious gubernatorial election in 1805 extracted the most vile and venomous attacks against the candidates originating from the journals. Thomas McKean would win re-election with the adamant support of the *The Tree of Liberty*. The vicious attacks escalated into personal threats.

In the Christmas 1805 edition, Pentland announced that Tarleton Bates and Henry Baldwin were *two of the most abandoned political miscreants that ever disgraced a State*.

On the evening of January 2, 1806, Bates reportedly encountered Pentland on Market Street. He was armed with a whip and struck Pentland with several lashes. Pentland reported the attack to legal authorities.

Bates responded by simply mocking his rival's cowardice.

Ephraim Pentland decided to taunt Bates further by challenging him to a duel. Dueling had been outlawed in Pennsylvania since 1794 with stiff repercussions. Participants could incur fines, imprisonment and even a loss of state citizenship. The more unfortunate rivals might not even survive the gunfire exchange.

On January 6, 1806, Pentland sent Thomas Stewart in his place to deliver the dueling challenge. Stewart was a young local shopkeeper and the son of a minister. Bates declined the challenge. He denigrated the messenger as simply an *apprentice* and *a man of no social standing*.

Pentland responded by circulating posters throughout the town branding Bates a coward.

Thomas Stewart took offense towards Tarleton Bates' tone and demanded an apology for himself. Not receiving one, the next day, he challenged Bates to a duel. Perhaps Bates anticipated that Stewart was an untrained marksman and an easy casualty. He accepted the challenge.

Throughout the drama, Ephraim Pentland was conspicuously absent. He was responsible for initiating the ritual, but unwilling to become a participant.

Bates and Stewart selected their seconds and the duel was promptly arranged for January 8. Accessing the Craft Park terrain involved rowing down the Monongalia River and strolling several hundred yards from the bank to a flattened grassy glade.

In the majority of instances, dueling might be hazardous, but was rarely fatal. Each man's seconds loaded the pistols with powder and a ball. Each participant stood back to back and then marched ten paces forward. They would then turn, aim and fire toward their adversary. The pistols were difficult to aim from a stationary position. Each participant sagely positioned their bodies in a sideways stance making them even more elusive to strike.

Bates and Stewart solemnly began. Each fired. Their shots missed errantly into the trees. In many instances, an unsuccessful shot was sufficient to conclude the dispute. Each man would have been regarded as defending their honor and substantiated their bravery.

Their first missed exchange did not conclude the contest. The seconds reloaded the pistols once again. The two men marched ten paces, steadied themselves and fired. Bates' shot missed again, but Stewart struck his opponent in the chest. Bates collapsed immediately and expired within the hour.

Mention of the shooting was downplayed in the *Pittsburgh Gazette*. Both men were lauded for following the *strictest rules of honor*. Bates would become lionized in the press as an *invaluable servant* and one of society's *brightest ornaments*. His funeral was the largest witnessed in Pittsburgh up to that time. He was buried with a simple marking next to the current Trinity Cathedral. The precise location has been obscured through history.

Thomas Stewart escaped to Baltimore and never returned to Pittsburgh. In the strangest irony, Ephraim Pentland became a protonotary as his publishing rival Bates had in 1808. He held the position for a decade.

Ideals, libel and senseless defamation prematurely ended the promising prospects of 30-year-old Tarleton Bates, Esquire.

**The Last Public Execution in Allegheny County
Gallows Site: Intersection Fourth Avenue and Grant
Streets, Pittsburgh**

John Tiernan and Pat Campbell had a contract for breaking stone on the Greensburg pike in the Turtle Creek district during late 1817. The men shared a cabin, but different temperaments.

Campbell was described as *inoffensive* and *sober*. Following work, he returned to his cabin and went directly to sleep. Tiernan preferred to unwind following his fatiguing labor. Turtle Creek Hill during that era offered a tavern, store and blacksmith shop. Tiernan began drinking. At some stage during the evening, he borrowed the owner's axe. He returned to his cabin and struck Campbell violently to death as he slept.

His motive for the killing was never publicly established. Tiernan attempted to flee his capture, but was apprehended during early January in Greensburg. On January 15, 1818, he was arraigned and two days later, tried and convicted of first-degree murder. He was sentenced to be hung on March 25. 1818.

The execution site was designated at the then head of Fourth Avenue where it emptied into Grant Street. The gallows were constructed in a terrain called *Suke's Run Hollow*.

Hanging day was described as *beautifully clear*. Thousands of spectators attended. They observing Tiernan transported from the jail yard via a cart. He was dressed in a blue coat with white pants and wore ankle-length laced boots.

Tiernan strode up to the gallows platform and was positioned atop the trapdoor. A noose was fitted around his neck. There was no published pleas or frantic utterances by the prisoner.

Sheriff Lazarus Stewart methodically cut the rope that supported the trap door. Tiernan dropped several feet and was left dangling. Once he was declared dead, the rope was disconnected from his body. He would be buried afterwards beneath the hangman's gallows.

His burial site is the current location of the One Oxford Center skyscraper. The setting became the site for a freak accident on Friday, July 1, 1983. Two window washers were suspended on the 34th floor when one of the cables attached to their working platform snapped. One would be rescued. The other plunged to his death.

The Great Fire of Pittsburgh That Destroyed A Third of the City
Concentration of Downtown Destruction: Boulevard of the Allies (North), Stanwix Street (Formerly Ferry Street/West), Fort Pitt Boulevard (Formerly Second Avenue/South) and Smithfield Street (East), Pittsburgh

On the morning of April 10, 1845, Ann Brooks stepped away from a newly fueled fire that she'd built to heat wash water. A spark from the fire ignited an adjacent ice shed. What should have been a relatively common blaze attracted immediate response from the local fire company.

When they directed their hose to extinguish the fire, *a sickly stream of muddy water* shot out. This result should have been anticipated. There been no rain for six weeks and the city reservoir was at a dangerously low level. Soot, dust and cotton fibers from industrial discharges had clogged the water storage source.

By mid-day of April 10th, gale force winds from the west spread the modest fire onto a nearby cotton factory and ultimately inferno. The bell from the Third Presbyterian Church sounded an alarm. The churches' stonewalls would save it from complete destruction. The wind shifted to the southeast and the fire began sweeping commercial structures block by block.

The Bank of Pittsburgh, presumed to be fireproof, was destroyed along with the famed Monongahela House. The hotel would later be reconstructed. One structure after another succumbed to the flames without pause. Despite the intensity of the blaze, it moved slowly enough to enable residents to escape and carry whatever personal possessions they could transport. Many fled across existing bridge spanning the Monongahela River creating chaos and congestion. The fire would later consume the bordering docks and warehouses.

The fire died down within the downtown at approximately 7:00 p.m. and two hours later in the factory district. Throughout the evening, periodic flare-ups would be accompanied by the sound of collapsing buildings.

The carnage had destroyed approximately one third of the structures inside the city. The area was estimated at approximately 60 acres. Only two people died from the fire. Afterwards, all of the local insurance agencies except one declared bankruptcy. Local ministers were quick to attribute the wrath of God for sinful behavior as the cause for the catastrophe.

Pittsburgh in 1845 had recently eclipsed its centennial of existence. The settlement was originally established as a French military camp at the confluence of the Allegheny and Monongahela Rivers. The city's growth and building planning since then had become erratic. The population was estimated at 20,000 residents.

The pollution from iron manufacturing had given Pittsburgh a universally disdained reputation. The walls of structures were smoke stained and the haze from the settling smog a lethal hazard. Life expectancy became far below the national average. Industrial workers were described by outsiders *as black as Satan himself.*

Following the clean up, re-construction began immediately. Property values skyrocketed. An estimated 400-500 new buildings replaced the former burned out debris. The damage from iron smelting however would require another century before controls became effective and noticeable.

**Monongahela House: From Historical Relevance to
Demolition**
Former Site of Monongahela House
1 Smithfield Street, Pittsburgh
Heinz History Center
1212 Smallman Street, Pittsburgh

Pittsburgh's first luxury hotel was the celebrated Monongahela House. The five-story facility featured 210 rooms, a 60-foot domed entryway, white marble floors and an elegant ballroom with gold gilded ceilings. Completed in 1840, the Monongahela was revered as one of the finest properties west of New York City and the Allegheny Mountains. The original structure would only last five years before becoming a casualty of the Great 1845 Fire. The hotel was rebuilt two years later.

The expanded Monongahela enabled the property to accommodate 300 guests. Throughout its storied history, the hotel hosted numerous luminaries including writers Charles Dickens, Horace Greeley and Mark Twain. Royalty such as England's King Edward VII and performers Lilly Langtry, Buffalo Bill, and Tom Thumb added to its prestige.

The hotel has a long affiliation with politics, particularly involving the Republican Party. In 1856, the policy-making caucus conducted their initial sessions at the hotel just prior to the 1856 Republican Party Convention in Philadelphia. The facility's hosting role has laid claim to its designation as the unofficial *birthplace* of the party.

American Presidents staying there have included John Quincy Adams, Andrew Jackson, Ulysses Grant, Benjamin Harrison, Grover Cleveland, and Teddy Roosevelt. Abraham Lincoln stopped overnight in 1841 en route to his initial presidential inauguration. He spoke briefly to an assembled gathering inside the hotel lobby following a delayed arrival.

He downplayed the threat of an impending war between the states that would prove erroneous only months later.

The walnut bed that Lincoln slept on within his private suite acquired a level of notoriety following his assassination four years later. Two subsequent Presidents, James Garfield and William McKinley, both from Ohio, would sleep in that same bed at the hotel. There exist speculative rumors that both men experienced bizarre dreams oriented around premonitions of death. Both men would later be shot to death during their term in office.

During the Civil War, the Monongahela played a pivotal role in providing sanctuary for runaway slaves. The *Safe House* status enabled slaves to hide and even modify their appearance as they headed towards Canada. Underground Railway associates misdirected slave owners from their pursuit by providing false directions and misinformation. The Abolitionist movement organized many of their strategy sessions at the Monongahela.

The last major renovations invested in the hotel were completed in 1906. Over the next three decades, conditions deteriorated. During the 1920s, the lavish ballroom was converted into a bowling alley and poolroom.

In 1935, the future of the Monongahela arrived at a crossroads. Plans to convert the property into the corporate headquarters of Jones and Laughlin failed to materialize. Left with few credible options, the complex was razed. A bus depot was constructed on the site. It has since been replaced by offices employed by the Allegheny County Human Services.

As for the cursed bed, its legacy continued briefly on display in a small museum in the South Park sector. Its next stop was the Soldiers and Sailors Memorial Hall in Oakland before finally settling into a level of permanency within the Heinz History Center. It is prominently staged on the fourth floor included with the Special Collections display.

The Barker Who Would Be Jailed Then Mayor
Market Square, Pittsburgh
Court House and Jail, 436 Grant Street, Pittsburgh

Joseph Barker was a vehement mid-19th century street preacher. He routinely appeared at *The Diamond* (today's Market Square) and denounced political corruption. His violent tirades and uncompromising temper drew large crowds and once prompted a riot on November 5, 1849. Mayor John Herron had him arrested and charged on three counts. The charges included inciting a riot, obstructing traffic and using lewd and indecent language in the delivery of incendiary theatre.

His formative origins were unknown and during his lifetime he never bothered attempting to clarify them. He was married with three children. He was described in public appearances as clean-shaven and well dressed in nearly always black attire. He was never without a neckcloth, stovepipe hat and long black cape.

The 44-year-old Barker's trial began on November 5, 1850 and became a contentious debate over the rights of free speech. On November 19th, he was found guilty and sentenced to a fine and 12-month jail term. Far from expressing remorse, Barker guaranteed vengeance against his adversaries.

In a measure, Barker succeeded. His supporters coordinated a mayoral write-in campaign for the approaching election. He won. He became sworn in as Pittsburgh's 17th mayor while incarcerated. His single 1850-51 term accomplished little in terms of local progress. Instead fiery speeches, debates and verbal exchanges simply polarized city government.

After his term expired, Barker attempted to regain the position. He would never hold public office again. In his fifties, he suffered the indignity of being decapitated in a train accident in the neighboring town of Manchester (now incorporated into Pittsburgh).

**Acknowledgement and Indifference Towards Composer
Stephen Collins Foster
Reconstructed Birthplace of Stephen Foster:
3600 Penn Avenue, Pittsburgh
Stephen Foster Memorial:
4301 Forbes Avenue, Pittsburgh**

The measure of an artist becomes the relevancy of their craft long after it has been disdained by the whimsy of fashion.

Stephen Collins Foster is often referred to as the *father of American music*. Many of his works have fallen into disfavor due to their racially lyrical overtones. His music reflected his era. He is considered in many circles an American tragedy who died destitute in New York City at the age of 37.

Foster was born in 1826 inside a modest cottage in Pittsburgh's Lower Lawrenceville district. He was the youngest sibling of six brothers and three sisters. The family suffered financially throughout his lifetime.

He enjoyed a diverse education in private academies yet had no formal instruction in music composition. He taught himself to play the clarinet, guitar, flute and piano. He studied classical artists including Mozart, Beethoven and Schubert.

The biography of Foster's early life and influences is scant. Many observers have indicated that his agent and brother Morrison Foster may have destroyed many documents that slanted unfavorably upon their family.

Despite living in Pittsburgh, a northern town, Foster's family did not support the abolition of slavery. Stephen would break with that tradition through his 1850s association with abolitionist leader Charles Shiras.

Foster became a prolific prodigy and has been credited with more than 200 published songs. That figure doesn't reflect his entire inventory. The majority of his handwritten music manuscripts have been lost and his actual output was certainly higher.

He wrote the majority of his best-known works in Pennsylvania, but frequently addressed Southern themes. He never lived in the South. His sole visit was during his honeymoon in 1852.

Among Foster's renowned works include *Camptown Races*, *Swanee River*, *My Old Kentucky Home*, *Jeanie With The Light Brown Hair*, *Oh! Susanna* and *Beautiful Dreamer*. Most remain hopelessly dated and affiliated with a lost cultural era. Odious blackfaced minstrels performed many of his works. These shows were popular entertainment outlets during his lifetime.

One may debate whether the racist overtones prevalent in his lyrics were a personal philosophy or simply popular pre-Civil War southern sentiments. Foster never clarified his intention or philosophy. He did stress an objective *to build up taste among refined people*. An appraisal of his work requires subjective interpretation. His publishing catalog credits, however, are the envy of any serious composer.

The last four years of his life were reportedly harsh despite his acclaim. He relocated to New York City living in squalor and declining health. Few accounts describe his living situation other than his correspondence via letters. His premature death became an immediate subject of extensive speculation.

The most widely circulated version of his death was that he'd become racked with fever during January 1864. Weakened by the illness, he'd fallen down in his hotel room in the Bowery district, somehow cutting his neck. He would die in Bellevue Hospital three days later. One eyewitness who was present with Foster when he died indicated that he was *lying on the floor, naked and suffering horribly.*

Other sources speculated that his declining fortunes had prompted him to commit suicide. When he died, his wallet contained a scrap of paper with the writing *Dear friends and gentle hearts* along with 37 cents in Civil War script. The significance of the *37* probably represented his present age.

In retrospect, it seems inconceivable that such an acknowledged talent could perish penniless, particular when a close family member managed his career. Foster's wife Jane would survive him until 1903 and his sole daughter Marion until 1935.

Further recognition towards Foster's body of work evolved posthumously. During the year of his death, iron manufacturer Andrew Kloman bought his original cottage homestead. He tore the structure down and replaced with a stately Second Empire architectural brick house. Fifty years later, steel mogul James Park purchased the house and gifted it to the city. Foster's daughter Marion was installed as the caretaker and taught piano lessons there until her death.

In 1934, automotive tycoon Henry Ford intended to buy what he assumed was Foster's real birthplace for his own museum of historic American buildings. Ford's representatives were convinced that Foster's actual birthplace was an old cottage two blocks further down Penn Avenue. Ford purchased that house and relocated it to Michigan. Twenty years later, his charitable organization admitted their identification mistake.

The reconstructed building suffered the indignity of municipal indifference for several decades. It was converted into a funeral home for twenty years until being bought by

American Wind Symphony Orchestra maestro Robert Boudreau. The property was converted into apartments and Boudreau's office space. He sold the property in 1997.

In 1937, the University of Pittsburgh opened the Stephen Collins Foster Memorial, an intimate performing arts center and museum. The building houses his collection of archives.

An additional local tribute honoring Foster was stationed on a pedestal in Schenley Plaza near the entrance to the Carnegie Museum of Natural History. The bronze sculpture initiated prolonged controversy and defacement throughout its public viewing history.

The work was commissioned and designed by committee in 1900 employing sculptor Giuseppe Moretti. The context is morbidly archaic and remains uncomfortable viewing. Foster is seated with a notebook in hand seeking his muse. A black slave representing *Uncle Ned* (one of his song titles) is strumming a banjo at his feet.

The mere existence of such a travesty raises the obvious question how it could have been approved and sustained during any era. The Pittsburgh Arts Commission rightfully removed the sculpture on April 26, 2018 following a unanimous vote. The fault behind its creation however cannot be attributed to Stephen Foster. He had already been buried nearly forty years before its creation.

Creative acclaim is capricious. Foster was acknowledged by the music industry, but scarcely financially compensated during his lifetime. Despite his contemporary lack of acclaim, he remains one of the few nineteenth century American composers still performed globally. Considering his works will soon be two centuries old, this recognition is substantial.

A Trail of the Blasphemed and Unfortunate
Dead Man's Hollow Conservation Area:
600 Scene Ridge Road, McKeesport

Dead Man's Hollow is considered one of the spookiest 400 acres of woodlands within Allegheny County. The nature preserve traces the Youghiogheny River outside of McKeesport. Litanies of legends, whether real or imagined, have fueled paranormal intrigue since the late 1800s.

The original moniker is traced back to 1874 when a man was discovered by a group of boys dangling from a noose. The body's decomposition made identification impossible. Some sources attributed the perpetrators as the Ku Klux Klan. Others have suggested the victim was Native American. Historical documentation has never substantiated the details.

George McClure was robbed at his dry goods shop in McKeesport in February 1880. He recklessly pursued the thieves into Dead Man's Hollow. He was gunned down. Nineteen-year-old Ward McConkey was convicted of the crime in August 1881. He protested his innocence right up until his hanging in May 1883. His last recorded words before an executioner's white cap was placed over his head were *Goodbye, murderers, goodbye.*

That same year on March 10th, a dynamite explosion killed four men at George Flemming's stone quarry inside the hollow. They were blasted when they attempted to thaw frozen explosives using an open flame. Predictably, the explosives ignited and the four suffered nearly immediate death. Another nearby man did survive with a severely burned face and body.

Another legend of more suspect verification involved a bank robbery in Clairton with the two perpetrators dividing the proceeds within the hollow. One double-crossed the other shooting him fatally. He then buried the cash clandestinely planning a return. He was sighted as he was leaving the woods and gunned down by law authorities. The money was never recovered and has stimulated the ambitions of treasure hunters for generations.

The lost treasure of Dead Man's Hollow may likely be as fanciful as a 30-40 foot massive snake that once patrolled the shade. Reports of sightings date back to the 1860s and a newspaper encounter was published in an 1893 edition. Neither the feared serpent, nor any descendants has since been documented. A popular theory is that moonshiners invented the tale to discourage curious poachers.

In 1887, Edward Woods, 74, was crossing the Youghiogheny River on the McClure Ferry when he lost his balance and fell in the waters. His body washed ashore near the hollow. The discovery of his cadaver seasoned suspicions of murder and haunting.

The final documented tragedy is verified. It concerned the untimely demise of Mike Sacco on September 25, 1905. Sacco was leaving his job at the Union Sewer Pipe Company when he pulled the rope to lower an elevator. It began to rise and Sacco leapt out attempting to reach the second floor. He nearly succeeded but his body became wedged between the elevator's floor and the second floor ceiling. He was crushed to death.

Dead Man's Hollow was once an important cog in Pittsburgh's industrial history. The preserve is a testament. Forgotten remnants of kilns, a P & LE Railroad water tank and several jutting concrete slabs are reminders of what once dominated the region. The Union Sewer Pipe Factory ruins are the most telling memory of an unsavory and sordid reputation. The building burned down in 1925.

ALLEGHENY LAND TRUST
DEAD MAN'S HOLLOW
Conservation Area
Keystone

The Railroad Unrest and Conflagration of 1877

26 Strikers Killed: Liberty Avenue at 28th Street, Pittsburgh

Union Railroad Station: Liberty Avenue at 11th Street, Pittsburgh

Pennsylvania suffered a rash of labor discord amongst railway works during 1877. Philadelphia, Reading, Shamokin and Scranton experienced strikes, but none matched the ferocity of Pittsburgh's.

The unrest was traced to repercussions following the national Panic of 1873. The consequences resulted in economic recession, reduced wages and increasing workload expectations.

On July 21-22, 1877, a malaise and fury erupted into protest and violence locally. Fifty-three individuals including women and children died with an additional 109 reported as injured. Many sources claimed the injury statistics were understated. Many participants involved in the uprising did not wish be identified or recorded as injured. They feared management reprisals.

The most prominent landmark, the Union Railroad Depot would be torched to the ground. It would be reconstructed afterwards. Thirty-eight additional buildings on the railroad grounds would be consumed by fire. One hundred and twenty locomotives and 1,200 rail cars were destroyed. The rail track damage ceased operations for a week.

Pittsburgh resembled a battle zone within the Strip District. Armed soldiers arrived into the city intending to lessen tensions and reinforce an appearance of calm. Their presence merely fanned the inferno of rapidly accelerating discontent between management and labor.

Angry railroad laborers, union agitators, the unemployed and even railroad property squatters fueled the protest movement.

The summer began sour. Railroad employees were obliged to accept a 10% pay cut that was implemented on June 1st. The superintendent of Pittsburgh's Pennsylvania Railroad office announced on July 19th a labor policy that modified operating trains. Double heading trains would become commonplace practice. This procedure would join two trains worth of cars into a single train with two locomotives. Additional crewmembers would not be added to accommodate the increased workload. The risk of potential accidents rose significantly.

One conductor named Ryan immediately refused to operate under these modified conditions with his crew. Twenty-five conductors and brakemen joined his protest. All were fired immediately. An additional replacement crew refused to operate his train. The contingent took control of the main track on East Liberty Street grinding traffic to a complete halt.

The rail superintendent and Pittsburgh's mayor were conveniently out of town. The public pronouncements by their temporary replacements were ignored. Kerosene was steadily dripping into a combustible environment. By midnight, the swarm of discontent had swollen to 1,400 participating strikers.

The following morning, efforts to disburse the protestors by law enforcement proved futile. Pittsburgh's Sheriff warned the crowd that his regiments were armed and would use force if necessary.

His resolve was unconvincing. His troops and other

accumulating militias had begun to side with the strikers. They refused to engage against the crowd. The unrest was mushrooming beyond simply a local dispute. The Pennsylvania National Guard and other troops began streaming into the city. They still remained outnumbered by protestors whose ranks were now estimated at 12,000.

Violence became inevitable.

On July 21 at 3:30 p.m. at the intersection of Liberty Avenue and 28th Street, the inevitable detonated. Pittsburgh's sheriff, his deputies and National Guard troops attempted to confront and disburse the crowd and arrest the protest leaders. They were met with scattered gunfire and hurled stones.

The parties co-mingled violently. Unarmed protestors attempted to wrest away rifles affixed with bayonets. A sickening ten-minute gun volley was initiated by panicking troops. Bodies of the dead and dying littered the streets. The protestors backtracked and regrouped. They resisted a second direct confrontation with the armed troops.

Chaos dominated the railroad grounds. Arson fires accentuated the mass hysteria. By 7:00 a.m. the next morning, looting citywide became rampant. The besieged fire department attempted to extinguish spreading fires extending along Liberty Street.

Unconfirmed rumors heightened worsening fears. One thousand miners were reportedly arriving en route intent on spreading broader disturbances. Shops remained closed throughout Pittsburgh.

Local armed veterans and national guardsmen created informal militias in a vain attempt to restore order. The dam restraining control had been breached. There were too many leaking holes to patch.

On July 28, Pennsylvania Governor Hartranft finally arrived with fresh militiamen from Philadelphia. They were accompanied by 14 artillery and 2 infantry units composed of federal troops. By then, the bedlam and radical passions had subsided. Railroad operations would resume two days later.

Afterwards blame was widely distributed. Railroad management was criticized for their indifference towards the strikers' concerns. Uprising leaders and participants were blamed for the extensive violence and property destruction.

Not everyone was distraught by the protest. Local organized labor groups became emboldened by their ability to mobilize quickly striking participants and sympathizers.

Pennsylvania's legislative committees exhibited perhaps the most deluded clarity of vision. These bodies completely ignored any railroad management culpability. Their unpopular policy changes were negated as a contributing factor towards the unrest.

The committees discovered the ultimate responsible blaming party. This group shared no lobbying voice, a diffused constituency and zero influence. The committee's findings conclusively attributed the protest movement to *tramps and idle vagrants*. The formerly forgotten railroad yard squatters were no longer ignored nationally either. U.S. Commissioner of Labor Carroll D. Wright labeled them *a volatile mix of poverty and anger*.

Eluding responsibility has remained consistent American political, labor and financial policy. The ability to redistribute blame was as prevalent following the 1877 railroad unrest as it remains in our current period of social media barbs and finger pointing.

RAILROAD STRIKE
OF 1877
In July, unrest hit U.S.
rail lines. Pennsylva-
nia Railroad workers
struck to resist wage
and job cuts. Here, on
July 21, militia fatally
shot some 26 people. A
battle followed. Rail
property was burned.
The strike was finally
broken by U.S. troops.
28th St

Founding Convention of the American Federation of Labor (AFL)
Former Site of Turner Hall *(Currently Mellon Center)*:
Smithfield Street and Sixth Avenue, Pittsburgh

During the 1880s, the nature of American industry was in the process of radical transition. Since the colonial era, skilled craftsmen had dominated the labor movement. Mass production was altering the terrain eroding many skilled trades.

In November 1881, representatives from a variety of local, regional and national union organizations congregated at Pittsburgh's Turner Hall. The 107 delegates met to form a new Federation of Organized Trades and Labor Unions (FOTLU).

The group was composed of skilled tradesmen including coopers, granite cutters, printers, iron and steel workers, cotton and wool spinners and seamen. Samuel Gompers, a cigar maker, headed the group. He had been a leading figure in craft unionism for nearly five decades.

His focus on skilled craftsmen splintered the group away from the Knights of Labor who preferred the inclusion of unskilled workers. In 1886, the Knights organized a peaceful rally at Haymarket Square in Chicago. A bomb reportedly planted by radical anarchists exploded sending organizers and participants into disarray. The Knight eventually dissolved from the adverse publicity.

Afterwards, Gompers convened a follow-up conference of trade unions in Columbus, Ohio. He merged his FOTLU with twelve other national unions to form the American Federation of Labor (AFL) composed of 140,000 members.

The AFL had minimal influence initially with Pittsburgh's

steel industry. Not until their affiliation with the Congress of Industrial Organization (CIO) during the Great Depression would they be able to represent and unionize steel workers.

**An Iconic Timepiece and Downtown Meeting Destination
Kaufmann's Clock:
400 Fifth Avenue, Pittsburgh**

Kaufmann's Clock is one of downtown Pittsburgh's principle iconic meeting and landmark locations. Named after the former Kaufmann's Department Store, the original timepiece was mounted in 1884 on a post installed outside of the store.

In 1913, the clock was relocated to its present location on one of downtown's major thoroughfares. The clock is fabricated primarily of bronze and weighs one and a quarter ton. Its last major cleaning occurred in 1987. The tarnished clock resisted an unsuccessful dosage of solvents, but equipment used to clean and polish bridges proved successful.

On January 27, 1917, the clock's resiliency was tested by a downtown inferno that ravaged Fifth Avenue. The fire reportedly started from unknown causes during the late evening in a corner of the McCrory Five and Ten Cent Store Building. A night watchman discovered billowing smoke at 1:50 a.m. and managed to stagger onto the street ten minutes later nearly overcome.

The flames spread quickly to the adjoining Frank and Seder's department store. Soon the entire eastern section of Fifth Avenue was engulfed. Roofs began to collapse and a brisk wind circulated the flames. The icy conditions made containing the blaze perilous with freezing water adding to the weight of building walls. The added weight collapsed some walls and flooring.

The 4-story Frank and Seder and McCrory Buildings would ultimately be destroyed. Adding to the casualty inventory were the Hilton Company clothing store, Grand Opera House and numerous retail stores and restaurants.

The Kaufmann's Clock survived the scare.

A more pragmatic threat to the clock's longevity arrived in 2006 when the Macy's department store replaced the Kaufmann's name. In 2015, that Macy's was shuttered and the building was sold to a developer. The developer has promised to retain the iconic clock outside of the building preserving the continuity of a Pittsburgh landmark.

WARNER
CENTRE

**A Fatal Cyclone Touches Down Within Downtown
Core Of Damage: 500 Block of Wood Street, Pittsburgh**
(Corner Wood and Diamond/Now Oliver Streets)

A cyclone ravaged western Pennsylvania at noon on January 9, 1889 touching down within Pittsburgh's downtown. Headlines covering the destruction itemized eighty factory women's deaths, extensive property damage and scattered losses of life.

Within the downtown corridor, a newly constructed four-story commercial building collapsed. C. L. Wiley owned the building. The force of that cascading structure became so extreme that the rear walls of the Rea Brothers and J. R. Welden department stores were crushed. Their front walls tumbled to the pavement below burying numerous people in the debris on the Wood Street side.

Hundreds of spectators, despite the extreme risk, assisted in extricating the buried. During the first four hours of the calamity alone, forty-eight people were lifted from the rubble.

The storm reportedly struck with *overwhelming suddenness*. The winds were accompanied by torrents of rain sweeping pedestrians and vehicles into a *mangled mess*. There is no record of a precise death toll. The catastrophe would serve as

a preamble for a far greater calamity that year on May 31st. That misfortune would be known internationally as the Johnstown Flood.

NO
TURN
ON RED
7AM-10PM
KWB-8674

An Apparition Inventory of Pittsburgh's Spiritworld
Pittsburgh Playhouse
350 Forbes Avenue, Pittsburgh
Carnegie Library of Homestead

510 E 10th Avenue, Pittsburgh
Chatham University's Woodland Hall
Fifth and Maryland Avenue, Pittsburgh
Frick Mansion
7227 Reynolds Street, Pittsburgh
Broughton Elementary School
935 Schang Road, Pittsburgh

Every established urban center has spirits, haunting and apparitions that linger amidst prominent landmarks and buildings. The older the structure...the more probable the sighting. The stories vary, but frequently are prompted by a premature or grotesque death of a foremost personage. In many instances, the building was a dominant presence in their earthly life and they simply do not wish to let go.

None of these spirits have appeared to age, particular if they were considered attractive during their mortal existence. Many encourage contact or interaction. Others prefer their anonymity and distance.

Pittsburgh is no exception to this phenomenon. The following are some of the most noteworthy if not plausible sites where phantoms still reportedly patrol the premises.

Pittsburgh Playhouse
A combination former brothel and subsequent church, the triple stage presentation center is owned and operated by Point Park University's performance art department. *The Lady in White* reportedly paces the balcony of the Rauh Theatre beseeching her dead husband's name.

John Johns was an actor at the Playhouse who suffered a heart attack on stage and afterwards expired in his dressing room, He is typically viewed in an audience seat wearing a tuxedo.

Carnegie Library of Homestead

One might easily presume that namesake Andrew Carnegie would roam the premises considering the main branch opened in 1895. One of the legends involves books that relocate themselves without human intervention. The most unnerving discovery to librarians is finding editions scattered on the floor after being properly shelved at closing time the night before.

A workman was once electrocuted while installing an electrical box in the basement. Each time that he has been sighted by a staff person or patron, he immediately vanishes. Since few or any patrons have access to the basement, his appearance is *employee exclusive*.

A judge who regularly frequented the library during the early 1900s decided without explanation to hang himself in the stacks. His body was reportedly discovered and removed for burial. Strange writings began appearing near the spot of his hanging noose. The messages were scribbled high on the ceiling at almost an impossible level for a human hand to reach. The cryptic writings were determined to be the same each time in Latin: *Sentio Est Hic*. The translation: *Judge Is Here*.

Chatham University's Woodland Hall

Situated in the midst of Chatham University, Woodland Hall was constructed in 1909 and has undergone numerous transformations and facelifts. *The Blue Lady* is the university's most spotted spirit and best known for startling Woodland Hall residents. She has been identified as roaming the halls in a stately blue dress and wandering into student's room. A companion ghost is a male child that periodically encourages students to play with him.

Frick Mansion
In 1882, the original mansion became the home of Henry Clay Frick and his wife. Frick earned his millions when his company began turning coal into coke, a fuel that the steel industry was dependent upon. The couple collected major works of art throughout their life together.

Two of their children died before the age of 7. Superstitious, the family would relocate to New York City seven years later with their two surviving children. The house remained uninhabited for nearly a century. Their youngest daughter Helen would become an avid art collector and in 1970 opened property into The Frick Art Museum to display the family's accumulated artworks.

Helen moved back into the family home to reside in 1981. She lived alone there until her death three years later. Her spirit reportedly haunts the house as evidenced by overheard third floor footsteps and depressions in the bed of her mother.

Broughton Elementary School
Constructed in 1929, the long-shuttered elementary school in the South Park district apparently has not graduated everyone permanently. The ghosts of mischievous children and their fatigued teachers remain on the grounds. Yelling, running and moving objects have typified the location's eternal recess.

A Christmas Eve Train Derailment Mars The Holiday Mount Washington Tunnel Near The Smithfield Street Bridge, Pittsburgh

The afternoon of 1917 Christmas Eve was seasonally frigid and stormy as 114 riders packed the Pittsburgh Railways streetcar #4236 along the Knoxville line. The passengers were predominantly workers, visitors and Christmas shoppers running out of time.

The trolley entered a tunnel at the South Hills Junction and its utility pole lost contact with the wire. The motorman from the trailing Charleroi car walked over to reset the pole. Lights and power immediately returned to the car.

The Car #4236 motorman was anxious to make up for the lost time due to the delay. He released the accelerating car to full speed as it headed down the tunnel's perilous incline. The car leapt off the tracks near the south end of the Mount Washington Transit Tunnel near the Smithfield Street Bridge.

The errant train sliced through a fire hydrant and two utility poles. It slid an additional 100 feet across cobblestones before crashing into an iron fence and settling in front of the Pennsylvania and Lake Erie Railroad terminal.

The carnage was devastating. One woman was disfigured so badly from the impact that she was never identified. Twenty-four people would perish including 17 women and girls. The accompanying injury count was extensive.

The transit tunnel remains operating over a century later. The 1917 derailment remains Pittsburgh's worst historical transit tragedy.

STOP

STOP
RR

Village Park and the Abrupt Collapse of the Armstrong-McKelvy Building
Second Avenue at Wood Street, Pittsburgh

Village Park is a landscaped environment fronting Point Park University's Frontier Hall. The square is nestled amongst numerous high-rise structures within the downtown core that are owned by the college.

Point Park University is a remarkable success story originating from modest beginnings. The institution has evolved into one of the largest investors of downtown Pittsburgh real estate.

The university began as a single-room business school called the *Business Training College* in 1933. Dorothy and Herbert Finkelor founded the institution serving 50 students specializing in business and secretarial classes. Over the subsequent decades, the school has extensively expanded their facilities and departmental subject matter offerings. Their performing arts program is recognized globally.

Village Park is a diminutive meeting space for pause and reflection featuring a prominent stone-sculpted fountain. The square blends seamlessly into the surrounding urban environment. Ironically it shares a tragic history originating during the initial year of the twentieth century.

In 1900, a four-story commercial building occupied the site. The structure was the corporate headquarters for the Armstrong-McKelvy Lead and Oil Company. On a Thursday workday afternoon, April 12th, the building abruptly collapsed without warning.

Three dead workers would be removed from the extensive rubble. The cause of the disaster wasn't revealed publicly, but one may presume it was based on shoddy construction. The extensively damaged structure would be demolished and never replaced.

There are no memorials acknowledging the building's former existence. Urban centers are historically reconstructed on the strata of ruined layers minus sentimentality. One day the Village Park parcel may become more financially advantageous to become an existing building extension or fresh high-rise construction.

The Biddle Brothers and Mrs. Soffel
Biddle Brothers Residence:
34 Fulton Street, Pittsburgh *(Renumbered or Destroyed)*
Allegheny County Jail:
Corner Ross Street and Fifth Avenue, Pittsburgh
Kate Soffel's Final Residence: 26 Southern Avenue,
Pittsburgh

During the first four months of 1901, twenty-seven burglaries were reported within Pittsburgh. Investigators concluded a single gang was responsible.

During the early morning of April 12, grocer Thomas Kahney interrupted a burglary of his store. He was shot to death by one of the thieves. Two police detectives, Robert Gray and Patrick Fitzgerald received a tip regarding a criminal gang lodging in the Manchester district.

The officers approached the reported house, but were denied entrance. They attempt to force entry and were met with a single gunshot. Officer Patrick Fitzgerald died from the shooting. A posse surrounded the house and then arrested the occupants. They included brothers Ed and Jack Biddle, Frank Dorman and two women.

The gang was charged with the burglaries and the murder. At their trial, the Biddle Brothers were convicted and sentenced to death. Their execution was scheduled for December 12, 1901. Dorman was sentenced to life imprisonment and the two women were acquitted and freed.

Immediate justice was temporarily suspended when Pennsylvania's governor granted the Biddle Brothers a 60-day stay on their execution. The pair was interned inside the Alleghany County Jail.

Living on fleeting borrowed time, the brothers desperately sought an outlet for escape. When they first entered the prison in early November, Ed Biddle cultivated an acquaintance with the warden's wife, Kate Soffel. Biddle was regarded as handsome and persuasive. Within a month, he had convinced her of his passionate affection. Her infatuation became mutual and inflamed. During the month of December, the pair began planning an escape strategy and the promise of a future life together in Canada.

Kate Soffel smuggled saws and two revolvers for the brothers during visitations. Her husband, Peter Soffel had been warned of her growing affection. He opted to ignore her indiscretion.

The brothers immediately began sawing their jail cell bars and plotting the proper moment to launch an escape. Their execution was eminent. Time was not their ally.

At 4:00 a.m. on January 30, 1902, the brothers launched their plan. Two guards were on duty that early morning. Ed Biddle shouted from his second level cell to prison guard James McGeary that his brother was violently ill. He requested cramp medicine immediately. McGeary complied. When he returned with the medication, the brothers overpowered him. They were able to expediently free themselves from their cell due to the severed bars.

McGeary was tossed over a railing sixteen feet below. One of the brothers shot the other responding guard. He was relocated to a prison dungeon where his shouting could not be heard. Both guards would survive their severe injuries.

The brothers lifted the prison keys from McGeary and strolled out of the institution onto Ross Street. Kate Soffel was waiting for them with a readied horse and sleigh.

Upon his discovery of the injured guards and prisoner escape, Warden Soffel comprehended the duplicity of his wife. Kate Soffel was the mother of four children, but she'd vanished with the Biddle Brothers. The warnings that Soffel had ignored were blatantly realized.

The daring escape dominated the local headlines. Images of the Biddle Brothers stimulated enormous interest amongst Pittsburgh's female population.

The city was blanketed in snow and the sole means of pursuit involved horse drawn sleighs. A posse of three police detectives and five other officers followed the fugitive's trail.

The brother's escape was doomed from the outset. They might have reached Canada alone expediently on horseback. One or both of them felt a sense of obligation towards their liberator. The trio was sighting sharing dinner on the evening of their freedom at the J.J. Stevens residence in Mount Chestnut, five miles east of Butler.

The next day, two miles from Mount Prospect, the posse closed in. As the lawmen narrowed their pursuit within sixty yards, they commanded the fugitives to halt.

The Biddle Brother's understood that their fate if captured was already certain. They responded with immediate gunfire. Both would be wounded multiple times in the ensuing exchange. Each rolled off the sleigh mortally wounded. Kate Soffel was shot in the breast and tumbled onto the snow. There would be speculation later as to who was the source of her gunshot wound. None of the pursuing officers were struck.

The wounded fugitives were transferred to a Butler hospital. On February 1st, Ed Biddle would expire at 7:35 p.m. His brother Jack died three hours later. Kate Soffel survived.

The brothers' bodies were transported back into Pittsburgh via train. They were prepared for burial at a South Side funeral home. An estimated 5,000 curious spectators would view them, the majority being hysterically weeping women. These same mourners followed the burial procession to Calvary Cemetery. The brothers were buried together in a single plot.

One distraught admirer, Mary Dale, 25, became so bereaved by her imaginary loss that she poisoned herself fatally. She had written to Jack Biddle pledging her undying devotion. Without Jack Biddle alive, she compromised on her wager with a heavenly reunion, provided either qualified.

Kate Soffel insisted publicly that she'd only become involved because she believed both men were innocent. An extensively penned letter written by her that authorities recovered confirmed that she'd *fallen in love* with Ed back in November. The letter also indicated that they'd begun preparations for their intended escape the following month.

Kate Soffel had felt suffocated in an unhappy marriage, but she reportedly hoped for reconciliation afterwards with her husband. Warden Soffel could not forget his public humiliation. He filed for divorce on June 28, 1902. In his declaration, he indicated that Ed Biddle was merely one in a series of his wife's prior infidelities. Even a cuckolded husband had limitations on his capacity for forgiveness.

Kate Soffel would serve a maximum two-year sentence for her role as an accessory in the dark tragedy. Upon her release, she altered her name and moved in with her sister at a Mount Washington neighborhood. Her notoriety made her an object of both empathy and ridicule. She attempted to reinvent herself and reconstruct her life as a dressmaker.

A popular play entitled *A Desperate Chance* toured regionally reenacting the escape adventure. In Cincinnati, Kate Soffel viewed a performance. She became incensed that her daughter's actual names were employed in the production. She obtained an injunction prohibiting the use of their names. Rumors circulated that her anger was fueled by not being cast as herself in the production.

The play was a curious monstrosity. The production featured the Biddle Brothers actual escape horse and sleigh. Local police donated the pistols and handcuffs used during the fatal gun battle.

Her brief infamy ended by the conclusion of the decade. She contracted typhoid fever and died on August 31, 1909 at the Western Pennsylvania Hospital where one of her daughters was a nurse.

The legacy of the deceased Biddle Brothers did not entirely dissipate upon their death. Prisoners at the Allegheny County Jail have complained about seeing their apparition roaming the halls since 1907. Kate Soffel's bedroom inside the jail later became an office for the Deputy Warden. Occupants have described ghost antics and frigid touches from the beyond.

Kate Soffel's brief sampling of forbidden passion, public notice and unconventionality would find a future audience in 1984. A motion picture entitled *Mrs. Soffel* starring Diane Keaton and Mel Gibson would be released that year to modest acclaim.

An Ill-Fated Marriage For A Title and Society Recognition
William Thaw Birthplace:
Wood Street Commons, 304 Wood Street, Pittsburgh
Marriage Site: Calvary Episcopal Church (*Demolished and Subsequently Replaced By A Target Store*)
6231 Penn Avenue, Pittsburgh

William Thaw earned his wealth from banking, steam canal boats, coal and railroad interests. He was born in Pittsburgh in 1818 and during his lifetime became considered one of the 100 wealthiest Americans.

He would marry a second time after becoming a widower in 1863. He fathered ten children, five from each wife. Two of his children from second wife, Mary Copley Thaw would ultimately create international front-page headlines. Each was conceived when he was past fifty.

Alice Cornelia Thaw was his youngest child. When William Thaw died at the age of 70 in Paris, she became an extremely wealthy heiress and desirable object for matrimony.

George Seymour was the second oldest child and eldest son born to Hugh Seymour, the 6th Marquis of Hertford. What George Seymour lacked in financial, ethical or business acumen, he compensated with an aristocratic title as the 7th Marquis of Hertford.

In 1895, he was sent to Australia due to his blatantly inappropriate behavior in England. He became infamous there for his riotous all-male parties, debauchery and dishonesty. As the manager of a family owned sugar cane and banana plantation, he was a failure. He returned to England in 1897 and served as a Lieutenant in the Warwickshire Imperial Yeomanry.

He was nine years older than Alice Thaw, but considered a sound strategic marriage partner. His title could open social doors that wealth could not. Alice expressed no overt reservations about her future groom prior to their marriage.

Seymour arrived in Washington D.C. as a two-week Thaw guest at a family rented residence on Lafayette Square. The couple's engagement was announced in February 1903. There were rumors that Seymour proposed to Alice only after her niece rejected him. The wedding would be postponed several times.

During his time on the East Coast, he blazed a wide trail of debt in New York City due to extravagant partying and gambling losses. None of these sordid details were disclosed before the scheduled wedding on April 27, 1903.

Seymour understood the leveraging power of his title and Mrs. Thaw's desire for admittance into English high society. Shortly before the marriage ceremony commenced at Pittsburgh's old Calvary Episcopal Church, he threatened to back out. He missed his rehearsal dinner. He extorted the Thaw family to increase the dowry.

The family complied, but their lawyers inserted legal protections into the text that would later haunt Seymour.

The wedding ceremony was a public triumph for the Thaw family. The marriage was an immediate disaster. The couple sailed aboard the *St. Paul* to England. The issue of his New York debts surfaced just before their departure. Seymour claimed that his father would settle any of his obligations and his creditors should contact the family lawyer. It is presumed that the debts remained unpaid.

Within a few months after their vows, Seymour reportedly *ill-treated* Alice. She tolerated their miserable arrangement until January 1908 when she sued for divorce. The marriage was annulled that same year on the grounds of sexual non-consummation. The divorce degree specified that all financial interests were to be returned to the Thaw family. The fine print from the modified dowry contract enabled this transfer.

Alice Thaw resumed using her maiden name and moved to Lenox, Massachusetts. She would remarry in March 1913 to Geoffrey Whitney, Sr., a Massachusetts stockbroker. The couple had two sons and no public drama. She died at the age of 75 in 1955.

Cut off from Thaw's fortune, George Seymour's life took a radical dive. For the next four years, he plunged into debt from his gambling losses and was forced to live in the attic of a London tenement. He declared bankruptcy in 1910 and became regarded as a social pariah by his former friends and acquaintances.

On March 23, 1912, his fortune abruptly shifted upward. Seymour would inherit fresh resources, property and titles upon his father's death. He became the proprietor of Ragley Hall. His former mere singular Marquis title proliferated. He was now officially the 7th Earl of Hertford, 7th Earl of Yarmouth, 8th Baron of Ragley, 7th Viscount of Beauchamp and the 8th Baron of Conway and Killultagh.

There was considerable speculation as to the extent of liquidity that accompanied his inheritance. In May 1913, he became engaged to Mrs. Moss-Cockle, a much older widow with a $3+ million fortune inherited from her deceased husband. By July, their fresh bloom of romance had withered and the engagement evaporated.

George Seymour would die quietly at his home in Torquay, Devonshire in 1940 at the age of 68. Remaining childless, his titles were passed on to his nephew Hugh Seymour. Hugh would marry the Comtesse de Caraman-Chimay and have four children together. He died from a brain tumor at the age of 67 on December 22, 1997.

TARGET
TARGET

A Fatally Overloaded Elevator Plunge
Donnelly Building
1030 Fifth Avenue, Pittsburgh (Renumbered From 1026)

On the evening of May 22, 1903, the Pennsylvania Electric Mechanical Institute hosted a party on the fifth and sixth floors of the Donnelley Building. Over 700 younger aged individuals packed the two upper floors. A ground level elevator was operating throughout the evening. The maximum load capacity for the car was between ten and twelve individuals.

As the festivities gathering momentum into the later hours, larger loads were being wedged in to accommodate the swelling demand. At 10:00 p.m., the elevator crammed with seventeen people departed the first floor bound for the sixth. Upon reaching its destination, the multi-ton cable abruptly snapped. The elevator began a free fall six floors before crashing into the elevator pit below.

The cable and assembly trailed the car landing on its roof and compounded the damage. Miraculously only four of the occupants were crushed to death. Their bodies were excessively mangled in the rubble. They couldn't be identified until the following morning and based only on the clothing they were wearing.

Fourteen occupants would survive including a 3-year old. The catastrophe might have been far worse. Several observers from the sixth floor nearly tumbled into the open shaft after they heard the noise being accidentally shoved by the accompanying panic. Overloading the elevator car was identified as the cause for the fatal plunge.

**A Cursed Railroad Bridge Vanished Into Oblivion
Wabash Bridge North Pier: Monongahela Wharf,
Pittsburgh**

Two ghostly piers on each bank of the Monongahela River are all that remain of the cursed Wabash Bridge. The span opened in 1904 transporting rail cars from the downtown Wabash Terminal to the Wabash Tunnel in Mount Washington. The objective was to compete with the firmly established Pennsylvania Railroad locally.

Amidst the two-year construction on October 19, 1903, an attempt to connect the two extremities of the bridge in the center failed. The center link collapsed resulting in ten construction worker's deaths. Upon completion in 1904, the line became immediately unprofitable and was declared bankrupt only four years later. In 1917, the Wabash railway line was absorbed into the Pittsburgh and West Virginia Railway.

The company continued to exploit the span until 1931. By then, it was limited to exclusively freight traffic that terminated downtown. A fire in 1946 destroyed the downtown terminal and warehouse rendering the need for the bridge useless.

Two years later, it was demolished and the steel used in the construction of the Dravosburg Bridge. The intact piers remain reminders of the bridge that couldn't financially float.

The Restless Soul and Debatable Sanity of Harry Thaw
Former Lyndhurst Mansion Parcel:
1165 Beechwood Boulevard, Pittsburgh
Marriage Site: Third Presbyterian Church
5701 Fifth Avenue, Pittsburgh

Thaw family heir Harry Kendall Thaw was patriarch William Thaw's first son from his second marriage to Mary Copley Thaw. During his lifetime, he would require nearly every dollar allocated to him from an estimated $400 million estate. The monies enabled him to afford a lifestyle of excess and salvage an existence he appeared bent on destroying.

The Thaw family occupied Lyndhurst Mansion completed in 1889, the year of William Thaw's death. The estate was located adjacent to Chatham University in the Squirrel Hill district. Three years following its completion, the structure became cursed by a tragedy accompanied by permanent haunting.

In 1902, a beautiful relative from Kentucky named Mary Thaw visited the family. During her stay, she rashly committed suicide in a large guest bathroom by hanging herself with a Turkish towel. No one was quite certain as to her motive, but her specter particularly tormented Harry Thaw.

Harry was already plagued by evidence of mental illness from his childhood. As he attained adulthood, his appetite for drinking, drugs, gambling and sex accelerated him along a hedonistic highway. His narcissism and recklessness cost the family substantial funds insuring damage control and to silence scandal. His most infamous action could not be publicly suppressed.

Evelyn Nesbit was considered one of the most beautiful women of her era. She became America's most popular modeling muse and the most recognizable *Gibson Girl*. She lost her virginity during her teenage years to an older Stanford White who reportedly plied her with champagne before raping her while she was unconscious. White was one of America's most renowned architects. He maintained a relationship with Nesbit even following their sordid encounter.

Evelyn Nesbit intoxicated Harry Thaw. He initially viewed her as a chorus girl in the Broadway musical *The Wild Rose*. He reportedly attended over forty performances. He arranged a meeting with her through an intermediary and steadily began showering her with gifts and cash.

Through an act of medical fate, he entered intimately into her affections and life. Nesbit suffered an emergency appendicitis. Under White's orders, she was transferred to a sanatorium for repose in upstate New York.

White and Thaw visited her regularly although never at the same time. Thaw continued obsessively showered her with gifts and affection. As their intimacy grew, Nesbit released her protective guard. She eventually confessed to him of her sexual violation by White.

Thaw became livid with his hatred towards White for stealing her virginity. White didn't care much for Thaw either and warned Nesbit against seeing him. He considered Thaw as merely a trifling idler squandering his family's fortune.

Thaw convinced Nesbit, with her mother as chaperone, to accompany him on a recuperative trip throughout Europe. He defined *recuperative* as a frenetic itinerary tiring everyone. His strategy succeeded in alienating Nesbit from her mother. The fatigue from the journey prompted mother and daughter to quarrel violently. Her mother finally remained in London separating from the couple.

Thaw continually brought up the subject of marriage. He shifted his tone and strategy. The remainder of their travels became a grueling inquisition regarding her relationship with White. In Austria, he booked the gothic Katzenstein Castle where he employed three servants in residence. He locked Evelyn in her room and reportedly launched a series of sexual assaults upon her including sadistic bondage. Throughout the entire ordeal, he stressed their need to marry. Following the abuse, he would become apologetic and upbeat.

Many wealthy men desired Evelyn Nesbit, but her revealed rape by White now made her less desirable as a marriage partner. She was desperate to escape her financial poverty. Following four obsessive years of pursuit, Nesbit finally consented to become Thaw's wife.

On April 4, 1905, the couple married at Pittsburgh's Third Presbyterian Church and moved into Lyndhurst Mansion. Life with Mary Copley Thaw for Nesbit became a cruel ordeal of subservience and psychological torture. Her envisioned existence of travel, leisure and entertainment became compromised since Mary Copley Thaw controlled the finances.

Thaw's obsession for revenge against White culminated on June 25, 1906. Thaw and Nesbit attended the opening of a musical revue that White had designed at Madison Square Garden. The couple viewed the entire spectacle together.

Afterwards, Thaw rose and casually walked towards White. He pulled out a pistol and fired three shots into his face. White dropped and died instantly. Thaw retuned to his wife and proudly announced that he had salvaged her honor. Hundreds witnessed the shooting in horror.

Thaw's celebrated two trials were the most publicized of the new century. He was certain that his vendetta would be understood and lauded. His confidence proved mistaken. He eventually pleaded *temporary insanity*.

Evelyn Nesbit testified supportively towards her husband. A reported financial incentive by the Thaw family encouraged her remarks. The financial figure was never disclosed but estimated at
$25,000. Some unqualified reports even suggested the figure at $1 million.

A jury found Thaw *not guilty by reason of insanity* and sentenced him to incarceration at Matteawan State Hospital for the Criminally Insane in Fishkill, New York. His wealth enabled him upgraded accommodations and privileges not available to other inmates.

During the initial trial, Mary Copley Thaw decided to disclose to the press about relative Mary Thaw's haunting of Lyndhurst Mansion. She was certain the apparition had prompted her son to commit the shooting. She vowed never to live there again and sold the property in 1907. Most observers felt the sale was actually conducted to free up immediate cash for financing her son's defense.

Thaw would unlawfully walk out of the asylum in 1913 and be driven over the border to Quebec, Canada. Following extended extradition negotiations, he was transported to the Mt. Madison House in Gorham, New Hampshire. He remained there during the summer of 1914 and then was transported back to New York for a sanity hearing. On July 16, 1915, a jury determined him sane and freed him.

Thaw and Nesbit divorced the same year as his release. Three years earlier, she had begun a touring stage act with modest success. In 1916, she married her dance partner Jack Clifford. Her notoriety became a both a blessing and curse. The curiosity factor stimulated sales, but Clifford eventually tired of being upstaged as *Mr. Evelyn Nesbit*. He left her in 1918 and they eventually finalized their divorce in 1933.

Her professional performance life would drift accompanied by periodic bookings due to her name recognition. She struggled with chronic financial problems, alcoholism, and morphine addiction. Her beauty became ravaged with age. There would be no reunion with fame for her. She died in total obscurity in Santa Monica, California in 1967 at the age 82.

Harry Thaw waited only a single year following his release before trouble resurfaced. He was charged with the kidnapping, beating and sexual assault of 19-year-old Frederic Gump at the Hotel McAlpin in New York City. Thaw fled to Philadelphia and attempted suicide upon being apprehended.

At his trial, he successfully reintroduced his previous insanity plea and was sentenced to confinement at the Kirkbride Asylum in Philadelphia. He was judged sane once again in 1924. A financial settlement between his mother and the victim's family was presumed.

Thaw scaled down his mania during later years residing in Virginia, Long Island and finally Florida. He died in Miami on February 22, 1947, ten days after his 76th birthday.

His estate had dwindled to $1 million. He would leave Nesbit with a bequest of $10,000. He denied paternity to a son named Russell that she claimed was his, conceived during a conjugal visit at the Matteawan Asylum.

The current site of Lyndhurst Mansion has only a street named Lyndhurst Drive to acknowledge its former existence.

The mansion was demolished in 1942. The original land parcel currently accommodates six houses.

In the afterlife, Harry Thaw's licentious character seemed certainly unsuitable for heaven. His eccentricities today might distinguish him as *celebrity worthy*. Perhaps he became an accepted candidate for reincarnation.

**A Ferocious Lion Attack At The Luna Amusement Park
Luna Park Former Property: Baum Boulevard (North),
Centre Avenue (South), North Craig Street (West) and
Melwood Avenue (East)**

In 1905, Luna Park opened in a North Oakland neighborhood on a 16-acre parcel. The amusement park featured roller coasters, picnic pavilions, carousels, a fun house, Ferris wheel, animal acts and diverse performance outlets. Electric lighting permeated during the evening hours consisting of 67,000 light bulbs. An entry façade featured an impressive moon themed design.

Luna Park was owner Frederick Ingersoll's initial theme park ground followed shortly by a similar version in Cleveland. The exorbitant expenses bankrupted Ingersoll by 1908. His park inventory was sold off, but the Luna Park name ultimately christened 44 distinct international facilities by the year of his death in 1929.

The Pittsburgh amusement park would close in 1909 upon the introduction of a more successful competitor Kennywood Park. There are no existing traces of the former Luna theme park within the parcel.

On August 27, 1907, the theme park generated unwanted publicity. A caged performance lion escaped and then sniffed out a picnicking group of women and children. They were part of a *Daughters of the American Revolution* contingent enjoying the grounds for the afternoon.

The errant lion emerged from behind a building. He sighted fifty-five-year old Anna Houck and selected her as his prey. The lion roared and sauntered towards her. En route, Houck pushed several children to safety. The lion overwhelmed Houck to the ground and began tearing at her clothing and flesh.

Spectators remained paralyzed with fear as she screamed. The chief of the park police arrived and emptied six rounds from his revolver into the animal with no apparent effect. The lion disdainfully continued to roar. He continued to paw and periodically lift up Houck, as she couldn't offer resistance.

Additional armed spectators arrived but fearing his hovering position over Houck fired at the ground near him hoping in vain to frighten him.

A police officer, George Sheridan mounted the roof of a bandstand and shot the lion in the head. He climbed down and confronted the wounded lion who backed off slightly. This hesitation enabled Sheridan to pick up Houck with one arm and relocate her out of immediate danger.

Confused, the lion resolved to attack Sheridan who was able to fire twice more. The second bullet shot from mere feet away dropped the lion to the ground.

The onlooking armed spectators then fired a barrage into the animal insuring his death. Anna Houck remained in shock from her injuries, but would recover.

The event was the second instance during 1907 that her surname *Houck* would make headlines news. A January 28th accident had a very different outcome. There was never published indication that either woman was related or familiar with the other.

Kate Houck of Pittsburgh was discovered deceased lying on a table inside her house by her husband. She had reportedly been *burned to a crisp*. The surrounding room, furniture and even the table itself displayed no evidence of fire damage.

Investigators concluded that she had died from spontaneous human combustion. The newspaper account detailed the unorthodox phenomenon as…*they are reduced to charred cinders and ashes by a fire that seemingly starts in or on them*. Their conclusion regarding Kate Houck's death would never be actually confirmed or contested from official sources.

A Folding Bed Suffocates An Exhausted Mover
Charles Murray's Former Residential Site:
6466 Penn Avenue, Pittsburgh

On March 3, 1909, Charles Murray, 39, spent the entire day moving his entire worldly belongings to his new residence on Penn Avenue. Exhausted from his toil, he and his wife opened their folding bed for an evening of repose. She would be the only one waking up the following morning.

During the late evening, the jaws of death were sprung shut upon the couple. Their bed enveloped them. Charles Murray would suffocate, while his wife escaped a similar fate. His improbable demise would fade into oblivion over a century later.

His former address is now part of the Bakery Square Complex bordered to the south by expansive apartment living complexes and high technology offices.

Folding beds have become as archaic as buttoned underbritches. Sadly…too late for the life of Charles Murray.

An Overloaded Passenger Ferry Sinks Into The Ohio River
McKees Rocks Bridge:
1000 Agnes Street, McKees Rocks

On a cool May 11th evening in 1909 nearing 8:00 p.m., a 24-foot long gasoline ferry was teetering crossing the Ohio River. Launched from McKees Rocks, the boat was headed towards the north shore. The skiff pilot was John Deer hired by the Albert Graham Company.

Deer made a fatal miscalculation. The ferry was overcrowded with 33 passengers crammed aboard. The majority had already worked overtime that day at the Pressed Steel Car Company. They were exhausted, impatient and famished. Disregarding safety concerns, they piled on board.

Deer overlooked the impending disaster and launched the ferry from shore. The craft immediately began taking in water. Midway through the crossing, conditions became unsupportable. The ferry would sink and toss its cargo at the approximate location of the current McKees Rocks Bridge.

Amidst the panic, few of the men were able to swim to shore due the heavy clothing they wore. The others rescued were plucked from the waters by arriving boats searching amidst the descending darkness. The steamboat *Tornado* scanned the Ohio River with its searchlights seeking additional survivors.

Twenty-four lives would perish. Their names are etched upon one of the concrete bridge columns memorializing the disaster. The McKees Rocks Bridge would be completed in 1931 making ferry service ultimately archaic.

The ferry catastrophe was not the sole calamity suffered by Pressed Steel Car employees that dreadful spring and summer. Working conditions had become lethal resulting in an average of one employee death per day.

Beginning on July 13th, a two-months strike was staged over the working conditions. The manifestation culminated in a violent confrontation on August 22nd. On that savage Sunday, strikers fought with management-hired private security agents and local police. At least a dozen participants were reportedly killed.

The Press Steel Car Company would weather that turbulent year in Pittsburgh. They ultimately ceased operations in 1956.

Remembrances of Origins Past
University of Pittsburgh Log Cabin
Corner Forbes Avenue and Schenley Drive Extension,
Pittsburgh
Mary Schenley Memorial Fountain
Schenley Drive, Pittsburgh

Appearing far out of continuity amidst the fervent construction pace of the Oakland district is a log cabin belonging to the University of Pittsburgh. The reconstructed cabin shares an obscured history, but is estimated to date between the 1820s and 1830s.

The structure was purchased at auction by a university trustee and donated to the institution. The cabin was then disassembled, transported to Pittsburgh, and reconstructed beginning in September 1986. Its location is adjacent to the Stephen Foster Memorial Center on the grounds of the Cathedral of Learning.

Part of the symbolism represented by the cabin is that the earliest classes at the university were conducted in similar structures during the 1790s. Its more utilitarian function today is to store salt for winter deicing.

One of the stranger commemorations honoring tradition and ancient mythology is the Mary Schenley Memorial Fountain titled *A Song of Nature*. Dedicated in 1918, the sculpture features two major figures. The God Pan is reclining comfortably and a straddling topless female singer rises above him playing the lute.

Their positioning reportedly *represents the yearly regeneration of all plant life*. Viewing the work from the right (or perhaps wrong) vantage point resembles a heatedly engaged eroticism between the pair. As Pan is the Greek fertility deity, the impression left by sculptor Victor David

Brenner is unlikely to be coincidental. Brenner is best known for designing the American Lincoln head penny still in circulation.

His choice of subject matter seemed an ideal image for the then scandalous honoree. Mary Schenley was the sole heiress for two wealthy Pittsburgh families. She eloped at the age of 15 with an impoverished 43-year-old captain in the British Army. She would live predominately in England, but redeem herself locally with her gift of the 300-acre Schenley Park in 1889. Time, money and generosity frequently erase perceived character indiscretions.

**An Industrialist's Architectural Vision and Near
Assassination
Union Trust Building:
501 Grant Street, Pittsburgh**

The Union Trust Building is a masterpiece of Flemish-Gothic architecture erected in 1915-16. Designed by local architect Frederick Osterling, the structure was built on the site of the former St. Paul's Catholic Cathedral.

Industrialist Henry Clay Frick financed the construction that was completed three years before his death. The Union Trust Company purchased the structure from the Frick estate in 1923 and remodeled the first four floors. The interior featured an arcade of 240 shops and galleries.

Architecturally, the design is noteworthy for its mansard roof with terra cotta dormers and two chapels appearing as towers. The interior is crowned by a central rotunda and stained glass dome.

The building would never have been constructed had an event from twenty-three years previously ended differently.

Henry Clay Frick was a complicated individual depending upon the prism from which he is viewed. He was a shrewd businessman, passionate art collector and very generous philanthropist towards the general public.

He was equally ruthless with his employees who'd generated his wealth. In June 1892, he slashed their wages, evicted workers from company housing and attempted to destroy the steel workers union. Amidst a subsequent workers' strike, he called in his private army of Pinkerton security guards to aggressively combat picket lines with violence. Ten of his striking employees were killed.

He didn't always get along with his business partners either. When he resigned from the board of directors of Carnegie Steel, Andrew Carnegie demanded that he sell his entire stock holdings from the company, even if below market value. The pair ended up in litigation.

Frick symbolized both the potential generosity and extreme worst traits of capitalism.

He was a man of habits and generally enjoyed a late lunch with friends and associates at the Duquesne Club. The building was a short distance from his corporate office at the Chronicle-Telegraph Building.

On Saturday, July 23, 1892, he had just returned to his desk following lunch when Alexander Berkman burst in. Berkman was wearing a newly fitted black suit. Avoiding introduction, he pulled out a .38 caliber revolver and fired two close range shots at Frick. One shot struck Frick's shoulder and the second his neck. Frick's associates wrestled Berkman to the ground. He fired a third unsuccessful round hitting the ceiling.

Failing with his gun, he reached for a dagger in his pocket, wildly slashing at Frick's legs. He was finally subdued and arrested. Berkman unapologetically confessed that his motive was to revenge the recent armed attack on striking workers. Frick epitomized all of the ideals that he detested and his attempted murder was a revolt to raise the consciousness of the working class.

His own philosophy mirrored the popular anarchist policies of that era. Adherents had become alienated by the American economic transformation from agrarian to industrial jobs. Industrial workers were often consigned to living in cloistered urban slums, working 12 to 16 hour shifts, and suffering from unhealthy workplace environments.

Berkman was no crazed or impulsive assassin. He had traveled to Pittsburgh days before his attack from Worcester, Massachusetts. He lived there with his mistress Emma Goldman. She operated an ice cream parlor. Goldman would later become one of the most celebrated revolutionaries and proponents of socialism during the early twentieth century.

Berkman would serve a fourteen-year prison sentence for his attack. Upon his release, he became renown for his anarchist beliefs through his writings and activism. He would accompany Goldman to Russia during the 1917 revolution. Both would leave disillusioned four years later over the terror tactics employed by the Bolsheviks. He continued his written works until the 1930s. He committed suicide in Nice, France in 1936 after suffering from extended ill health.

Frick's Chronicle-Telegraph building would be demolished in 1963 to make way for the construction of the US Steel Tower, the tallest skyscraper in Pittsburgh. The Union Trust Building has undergone several ownership transitions and was extensively restored in 2016.

A Catastrophic TNT Blast Following Ignored Orders
Former Aetna Chemical Facility
Noblestown Road, North Fayette Township

In 1916, an explosion at the Aetna Chemical Company's TNT manufacturing plant in Oakdale killed five employees. The incident would become a preamble to a more devastating blast two years later. Residents who lived near the facility had chronically complained about safety conditions at the facility that were being disregarded.

Dynamite is an obvious fragile composition with potentially catastrophic consequences. At noon on May 18, 1918, the local resident's worst fears were realized. A room where chemical were mixed inside the facility exploded. A series of subsequent blasts triggered a massive fire throughout the building.

The roof of the structure was lifted and entirely severed from its framing. After elevating slightly, it crumbled apart in scattered directions. Smoke and flames engulfed the interior and formerly sturdy metal supports were hurled in errant directions.

One hundred and ninety-three people would die in the catastrophe. Reportedly only half could be identified based on the ferocity of their incineration. The TNT was being manufactured for the Allied war effort during World War I. Aetna had ignored a demand by the federal government to cease using a specific volatile chemical in their mixture.

The company would escape accountability. The plant would close permanently six months following the explosion.

**The Construction Signing of Czechoslovakia
Loyal Order of Moose Building Site:
628-634 Penn Avenue, Pittsburgh**

By September 1918, World War I was nearing its conclusion. The Habsburg monarchy, the ruler of Austro-Hungary was nearing collapse. Their choice of siding with the Central Powers of Germany and the Ottoman Empire during the conflict proved catastrophic.

Fresh European national boundaries were destined to evolve. Fifty years preceding the war, nearly one million individuals of Czech and Slovak ethnicity had migrated to the United States and other nations. Their future return home would be orchestrated via nationalist groups operating within the United States.

The plans for an independent nation following the dissolution of Austro-Hungary were formed and refined within Cleveland and Pittsburgh. On Friday, May 31, 1918, delegates met at Pittsburgh's Moose Hall building under the leadership of Tomas Masaryk to sign an agreement. That document specified the nature and parameters of the future Czechoslovakian provisional government. This treaty would become known as the *Pittsburgh Agreement*.

The nation of Czechoslovakia would be finalized in October 1918 upon declaring its independence from Austro-Hungary. Tomas Masaryk would become the first President. During World War II, the country would be divided between German occupied territories and Allied Force controlled lands. Following the war, the nation became part of the eastern bloc ruthlessly governed by the Soviet Union.

The fall of the Berlin Wall and subsequent collapse of the Soviet Union reconciled the country to its former independent status. That reconciliation would be brief. In 1993,

Czechoslovakia split into two sovereign nations, the Czech Republic and Slovakia.

Czechoslovakia as a nation no longer exists. The Moose Club building has been demolished. The sole remembrance of the historic meeting and signing is a memorial sign located on the former fraternal building site.

A Heinz Family Legacy and Failed Attempt to Thwart An Ethnic Genocide
Heinz Historic Business Complex:
South Canal Street (North), River Avenue (South)
Chestnut Street (West) and Progress Street (East),
Pittsburgh

Henry John (H. J.) Heinz was born and raised in Birmingham, Pennsylvania to parents of Bavarian heritage. At the age of 25, he co-founded a small horseradish, sauerkraut, vinegar and pickle company in outlying Sharpsburg. It would fail six years later. He rebounded with a second business venture that extended into tomato ketchup and additional condiments. The H. J. Heinz Company would ultimately evolve into an international food conglomerate.

By 1888, the company had expanded to an extent that he could comfortably buy out his co-investing brother and cousin. The company's distinctive slogan *57 varieties* was introduced in 1896 by the time the company was already selling more than 60 product lines. Five was his favorite number and seven his wife's.

He leased buildings until 1890 when he staked his permanent headquarters in Pittsburgh. In 1884, he purchased several vacant lots on the north bank of the Allegheny River in the Troy Hill district. Construction began on twenty buildings from 1888 through 1906 of wood and beam construction.

Between 1906 through 1930, new buildings were constructed with steel beams and bricks reflecting Heinz's Romanesque Revival styling preferences. Constructions continued throughout the 1930s and 1940s as many of the older structures were demolished and replaced by contemporary industrial styles.

H. J. Heinz distinguished himself amongst the majority of his high-profile peers by his ethical business practices. He reportedly treated his workers well and legitimately earned their esteem and respect. His food industry peers and competitors did not necessarily share this commendation.

Amidst the horrific food scandals of the early twentieth century, Heinz lobbied extensively for passage of the Pure Food and Drug Act of 1906. The statute's passage ultimately created the U.S. Food and Drug Administration.

Heinz was a devout Christian and worshipped in various Protestant denominations. His commitment towards a living an exemplary life of responsibility and charity was passed along to his eldest son Howard.

Howard Heinz was sent by President Woodrow Wilson to the Middle East to coordinate famine relief efforts at the conclusion of World War I. On May 14, 1919, the day his father died at 74 from pneumonia, he oversaw the distribution of 30,000 tons of food into the region.

During this visit, he also witnessed the unfolding of a genocide obliterating local Armenians. Within harsh and remote areas of eastern Turkey and Armenia, Armenian citizens were being slaughtered daily by Turkish soldiers.

In a dispatch to Wilson, Heinz reported the carnage and urged him to send American troops to halt the slaughter. Despite his family's political influence, prestige and history of public service, Wilson did nothing. Heinz's pleas were ignored. An estimated 1.5 Armenians would be murdered in a catastrophe the responsible nation still refuses culpability for.

Wilson was too engrossed then with promoting his League of Nations proposal and basking in the acclaim lavished upon him during his December 1918 visit to Paris. His efforts at permanently eradicating war had earned him the 1919 Nobel

Peace. The attention clouded his judgment regarding an obscure killing field in a far away continent. He also disregarded the indifference domestically towards his international peace institution.

His euphoria became short-lived. American entrance into the League of Nations failed to pass through a US Congress vote. Wilson's idealism had swiftly evaporated. He had intended to run a third term to resuscitate his program appealing to the American public. In October, he suffered a major stroke that left him incapacitated. His presidential term officially expired on March 4, 1921. He would linger in disillusionment until his death at 67 on February 3, 1924.

Howard Heinz's meaningful attempt to influence American foreign policy proved insufficient.

The Heinz family generational successors have mirrored the successes and failures of many influential and dynastic American families. Members have been composed of an odd assortment of philanthropists, reckless tycoons, art patrons, alcoholics, educators and even politicians. The family has experienced schisms of estrangement and numerous courtroom battles concerning money. Scandal and tragedy has periodically intruded.

Family members no longer manage the H.J. Heinz Company and reportedly own less than 4% of the company's stock.

In 2001, the Heinz Corporation owned significant underutilized real estate within their corporate complex. Many of the historic buildings had been vacant for 5-8 years. With no long-range plans for their use, these storied edifices were sold to a residential developer and converted into lofts and apartments. Additional buildings have subsequently been sold off for additional commercial and residential uses.

**A Hillside of Bigotry Descends Upon Carnegie
Klansman Concentration: Chartiers Creek at Main
Street, Carnegie**

The origins of the Ku Klux Klan were initially distinctively a southern American states phenomena. Following their defeat in the Civil War, Tennessee veterans of the Confederate Army organized in 1865 in opposition to incoming northern political officials labeled *carpetbaggers* and freed slaves.

This movement of concentrated hatred prevailed during the reconstruction post-war era. President Ulysses S. Grant approval of the Enforcement Act in 1871 strengthened the federal government's powers to enforce the 14th and 15th Constitutional Amendments.

Membership in the Klan waned. Bigotry however wasn't eliminated.

The Klan movement resurrected in Atlanta during 1915 and subsequent waves of membership growth expanded into even extremities such as Portland, Oregon. The focus expanded beyond simply racial intolerance to include immigrants, communism and the Catholic Church.

In 1922, Hiram Wesley Evans, a Texas dentist, was elected as the national Imperial Wizard. Evans had grandiose visions regarding popular expansion for an unpopular movement. Evans rationalized that regionally murdered members could be enshrined as martyrs. This level of commitment might serve as a marketing bonanza. He did not volunteer himself to be amongst the martyrs' ranks.

Evans decided upon Carnegie as his Pennsylvania based rally destination. Carnegie is a Pittsburgh southwestern suburb with a significant immigrant Catholic population.   He'd likewise selected his martyr, local prominent Klan member Harry MacNeel.

During the afternoon of August 25, 1923, a rally was staged on Forsyth farm overlooking Carnegie. An initiation of new members ceremony inducted supposedly one thousand fresh recruits.

Awaiting the Klan below in Carnegie were large groups of protestors. City officials fearing the incendiary nature of their commingling refused the Klan a parade permit in the town.

With night descending and their rituals complete, the assemblage estimated at 10,000 was frothing for confrontation and violence. At 9:00 p.m., a 60-foot high cross was lit on the hillside accompanied by fireworks.

Members fumed over the local rejection of their parade permit. Several began interrupting Grand Wizard Hiram Evan's speech and demanding action. Despite his hesitations and without his permission, the gathered assemblage stormed into Carnegie with designated martyr Harry MacNeel leading. They crossed a bridge over Chartiers Creek and congregated on Main Street.

Amidst the chaos, a member of the group was felled by gunfire. Instead of MacNeel, a recent young inductee named Thomas Abbott was murdered. The parade quickly dissipated following the shooting. Local undertaker, Patrick McDermott was accused by Klan members of the killing. A coroner's jury would later acquit him.

The national organization's momentum steadily declined over the balance of the decade. Several chapters were closed due to financial irregularities practiced by their leadership. Numerous disgruntled Klansmen quit out of disgust realizing the movement was strictly a financial fundraising con game.

Sadly, their departure wasn't based on any insightful rejection of the hatred the organization espoused.

The Klan's attempt towards establishing a Pittsburgh foothold was aborted. The city's integration of divergent nationalities, cultures and religions proved inhospitable to divisive rhetoric.

Thomas Abbot never achieved martyrdom. He became pitied as simply a misguided and unsolved murder victim.

A Twenty Minute Fire Destroys A Local Iconic Crossing

Replacement Bridge: David McCullough Bridge (16th Street Bridge), Pittsburgh

On April 23, 1918, fire destroyed the covered wooden bridge that was known as both the 16th Street Bridge and the Mechanics Bridge. The original crossing had dated back to 1838, but its wood composition made it vulnerable to fire. A passing locomotive emitted sparks that ignited the wood framing. Within twenty minutes, the span was a charred and floating wreckage drifting along the Allegheny River.

In 1922, a replacement 16th Street steel trussed arch bridge opened. The span measured 1,900 feet in length with a width of 40 feet. The bridge has since evolved into one of Pittsburgh's most popularly traveled. Its longevity faced perceived peril as a consequence of the local 1936 St. Patrick's Day Flood.

Reports circulated that the bridge had collapsed due to the rising record-breaking floodwaters. Pittsburgh's police chief ordered all bridges closed for fear of damage caused by receding waters and floating debris. The rumors proved to be false and the accompanying panic-based decision ill advised.

On July 7, 2013, the 16th Street Bridge was named after Pittsburgh native, historian, author and television commentator David McCullough.

**A Globally Famed Actress Expires Inside a Pittsburgh Hotel Suite
William Pitt Union *(Formerly Schenley Park Hotel)*,
University of Pittsburgh:
3959 Fifth Avenue, Pittsburgh**

Eleonora Duse was considered one of the finest actresses of the late nineteenth and early twentieth centuries. Italian born, she was often compared with celebrated actress Sarah Bernhardt. She gained her initial success touring Europe during the 1880s. She followed that triumph with additional tours in South America, Russia and the United States. Her performances from the works of playwrights Henrik Ibsen and Gabriele d'Annunzio elevated her into then legendary status.

Duse achieved a celebrated power of conviction and truth on the stage through an intense absorption of her character. It remains a distinguishing genius amongst even today's famous performers. Her acting was considered purely intuitive and spontaneous, but those who knew her best confirmed of her intense labor to create that impression.

Duse's life was as fiery and passionate as her performance roles. She had affairs with renowned performers, artists, writers and dancers, including a widely speculated liaison with Isadora Duncan.

Throughout most of her adult life, she suffered from heart aliments. Her extensive years of touring further eroded her health. She retired from acting in 1909 and made a single silent film entitled *Ashes* during 1916. She loathed the production and quality of her performance.

In 1921, she returned to the stage and two years later became the first woman to be featured on the cover of *Time Magazine*.

In spring 1924, Pittsburgh was simply an eastward return leg venue for one of her touring productions. She contracted pneumonia locally and attempted to recuperate in Suite 524 of the Hotel Schenley. At 65, she was no longer as resilient to illness. On April 21, 1924 she expired inside her hotel room.

Her body was immediately transferred to New York City where she lay in state for four days prior to a funeral service. The body would then be returned to Italy for an additional memorial. She was buried in Asolo, Italy at the ceremony of Sant' Anna.

Amidst her prime, Duse was painted and photographed by the most renowned portrait artists. In 1947, a biographical film was released entitled *Eleonora Duse*. The once celebrated name *Duse* is sadly scarcely mentioned today amongst the ranks of elite actresses. Another famed actress of another era, Lillian Russell once resided inside the property in room 437. Her former residence is currently used as the offices for *The Pitt News* accompanied by stories that her spirit hovers and inspects editing proofs.

Other legends have emerged from the history of the hotel including a Russian prima ballerina who overslept a performance while drifting to sleep in the Tansky Family Lounge (the current lobby). She was so ashamed and humiliated by being replaced by her understudy that she took her own life that same evening.

On July 12, 1950, a hotel security guard went on a shooting spree that killed two men and wounded another. A motive was never determined for his outburst.

The once prestigious Hotel Schenley fell into disrepair and neglect and was sold in 1956 to the University of Pittsburgh. The facility currently serves as the student union building on campus. The drama remains continuous, but on a far more subdued scale.

A Skinny Building Born As An Act of Defiance
Hendel Building:
241 Forbes Avenue, Pittsburgh

Defying conventional logic and space limitations, fruit vendor Louis Hendel purchased a diminutive strip of land in 1918 along Forbes Avenue. At the time, he was operating his own business there inside a modest shack. The previous owner had been tycoon Andrew Mellon who'd purchased the property in 1907. Hendel was one of three tenants squeezed within the space. A cigar stand and restaurant occupied the remainder.

The small parcel had been reduced in width during 1903 amidst a street-widening project of Forbes Avenue (then called Diamond Street). The project was designed to ease vehicle and pedestrian traffic congestion. The alternation severed the width of the lot markedly to six feet. The length remained the previous standard sized 80 feet.

Before and especially after Hendel's acquisition, there remained major congestion issues. Customers from Hendel's fruit stand spilled out onto the street causing sidewalk obstructions. Hendel remained defiant towards the protests from neighboring business owners, the press and civic authorities.

Rather than compromise or create sensible alternatives to his created space dilemma, Hendel reacted in spitefulness. In 1926, he constructed a three-story structure within the tiny confines. The building is commonly referred to as the *Skinny Building*.

The structural curiosity attracted both fascination and criticism locally. Hendel renewed the existing leases with his two tenants and continued operating his fruit stand. He promoted the edifice as the *world's narrowest building* even though technically, the Sam Yee Building in Vancouver, Canada is a few inches less on the ground floor.

In 1928, the *Lincoln Restaurant* occupied the second and third floors. Their layout consisted of a row of narrow tables lining one wall. It became one of Pittsburgh's few dining establishments serving black customers. Initially the novelty of the location attracted a stable clientele. By 1931, the business failed.

Numerous commercial ventures would follow, but the space constraints made practicality impossible. The two upper floors in recent years have been consigned primarily as art exhibition showcases.

The most enduring tenant became a lunch counter called *Raywell's* that operated from 1938 to 1979. Patrons sat on stalls with their backs to the street, facing a narrow service counter. Waitresses were unable to pass each other from the inside. A grill was stationed in the corner.

Since the closure of *Raywell's*, several enterprises have operated within the confines. In 2021, PNC Financial Services, an American bank holding company purchased the structure and the adjacent Roberts Building.

IVERSAL

A Springtime Anti-Liquor Crusader Who Wilted By Autumn
William L. King's Residence: Webster Hall Apartments
101 North Dithridge Street, Pittsburgh
Castle Gardens Speakeasy:
655 Penn Avenue, Pittsburgh

Amidst the darkened era of rampant criminality within Pittsburgh, a brief redemptive hope arrived from Kansas City during early 1927. William L. King had effectively impacted crime there with his Anti-Saloon League.

King was given the title of Executive Secretary of the Citizens' Committee of Pittsburgh. Initially upon his arrival, the described *bespectacled and owlish-looking* man recruited members for the league. He spoke and appeared on behalf of the organization before churches and local social groups. Most observers dismissed him as an insignificant presence.

His perception altered radically in the spring when he suddenly appeared publicly armed with search warrants and federal agents. He began directing invasions on speakeasies and gambling establishments. The succession of raids resulted in the indictment of 77 individuals. A perceived cleanup movement seemed significantly underway. William L. King became a notable and feared presence.

King's momentum stalled in June when three of his investigators stormed the Castle Gardens, a notorious Hill district cabaret. The raid had been anticipated and the three were beaten viciously. The worst beating was directed towards investigator, Herman Steubenrauch who was later learned the source of the tip. Steubenrauch was reportedly on Police Superintendent Peter P. Walsh's secret payroll.

Walsh became very uncomfortable with King's publicized successes. He sought to discredit King and destroy the evidence he had accumulated. He ultimately was successful with both agendas.

In late July, King abruptly disappeared from his Webster Hall accommodations. Days afterward, many sources became convinced that he had been kidnapped. A letter arrived reportedly signed by King addressed to Pittsburgh newspapers. The text indicated that he was resigning his position from the Citizen's League *because he found its purposes were political.*

The head of the League doubted the legitimacy of the letter. King was located in Kansas City by a newspaperman via phone. King confided that there had been an attempt to blackmail him and he'd returned to his home in Kansas City *to combat them.* He added that he'd become recently married and feared that his name would be blackened to his new wife.

His version of events would become ultimately disputed upon his return to Pittsburgh under the guard of federal officers. He explained to the Citizens' League leadership why he had abruptly skipped town. The details of that explanation were never made public.

One of his statements would initiate immediate legal follow-up. King admitted accepting $300 from a gambling organization to leave town and drop prosecution efforts against them. He justified accepting the funds because he needed to return home quickly to recruit character witnesses for the anticipated blackmail attempt.

He fingered the sources of the payoff as gambling front man Jakie Klein and Police Superintendent Walsh. Both would be indicted together with charges of trying to tamper with a Federal witness. Walsh would be indicted later in 1929 on a wider range of charges involving police corruption.

King might have been reinstalled to his crusader status, but several inconsistencies lingered. Instead of a $300 payoff, Jakie Klein insisted the actual amount was $22,500. Worse, during autumn when the various criminal perpetrators came to trial, most of the charges against them were dismissed.

King vanished once again after hastily signing a confession that he had faked evidence in many of the raids. He would never return. His two affiliate agents would be arrested. The clean up and reform movement collapsed. Tainted money and bribes once again proliferated locally without restraint. Pittsburgh remained for sale to the highest bidder.

**Pittsburgh's Controversial Blue Laws
Soldiers & Sailors Memorial Hall:
4141 Fifth Avenue, Pittsburgh
Former Syria Mosque Site:
4400 Bigelow Boulevard, Pittsburgh**

The Sabbath Association of Allegheny County was never known for compromise. Most members were considered humorless enforcers of an archaic law. They rigidly notified authorities about any suspected violations of Pennsylvania's *Blue Laws*. These statues prohibited public activities, organized sports or commerce on Sundays. The laws had originally been enacted in 1794, but rarely were challenged.

In the eyes of proponents and the Sabbath Association, exceptions were unforgivable. Sunday was regarded to them as a day consecrated for worship and rest.

Sunday, April 24, 1927 would become a major test towards the validity of a law many perceived as antiquated. The Pittsburgh Symphony Orchestra had disbanded in 1910 due to a financial crisis. The hiatus stretched into 16 seasons before the Symphony Society re-formed in 1926. They announced plans to perform Sunday concerts at the Syria Mosque to inaugurate their new season.

The Sunday performances were necessitated and convenient because their musicians worked other jobs during the weekdays. Performance attendees arrived primarily from the suburbs.

The Syria Mosque was a 3,700-seat performance venue located next to the Soldiers & Sailors Memorial Hall. The Shriner Hall was constructed in 1911 and renowned as one of the finest examples of exotic revival architecture. The auditorium featured internationally renowned music performers, political rallies and speeches. Despite efforts to save the building as a historic landmark, the structure would be demolished on August 27, 1991.

The April 24th performance was packed to capacity. Uniformed motorcycle policemen guarded the entrance anticipating outside protests. Attendees felt that their defiance was a noble cause.

The performance began with an invocation requesting *tolerance and forbearance*. The repertoire included Weber's *Euryanthe* overture, Beethoven's 7th Symphony and two works by Peter Tchaikovsky. The audience was appreciative and applauded loudly following each number.

The Sabbath Association wasted no time the following day filing complaints before a district judge. Ten representatives of the symphony were singled out, found guilty, and fined $25 each. The decision was appealed and concerts continued on the previously scheduled Sundays. In July 1928, the State Superior Court tossed the case off the docket and overruled the fines.

The Sabbath Association remained outraged and steadfast. Prevailing secular interests had apparently doomed their cause. The struggle to liberate Sundays continued vigorously over the next several years. In 1933, supporters of professional sports successfully lobbied the legislature to allow individual cities to decide what leisure activities could be held on Sundays.

In Pittsburgh, voters passed an ordinance effectively disabling blue laws. The Pittsburgh Symphony and Pirates (later Steelers) football team were liberated to perform without fear of municipal interference, fines or arrest.

**The Four-Year Mob Reign and Violent Demise of the
Monastero Brothers**
Luigi *Big Gorilla* Lamendola Murder Site:
27 Chatham Street, Pittsburgh *(Currently Marriot Hotel)*
Stefano Monastero Murder Site:
**Former Saint John's Hospital Site: 3339 McClure Avenue,
Pittsburgh**
Joe *The Ghost* Pangallo Residence:
805 Eighth Street, McKees Rocks
Sam Monastero Murder Site:
Jacks Run Road near Balsam Street, Pittsburgh

Prohibition became a lucrative enterprise for certain Pittsburgh criminal families upon its 1920 introduction. The local mob had operated historically from loan sharking and gambling enterprises. Several elements contributed towards the desirability of illegal liquor distribution.

Prohibition statutes were widely unpopular locally. Males who had returned home from the trenches in France during World War I found the restrictions oppressive. Drinking laws became nearly impossible to enforce, particularly when local police departments and railroad porter networks were often primary sources of distribution. The demand never slackened and as bootleg alcohol products improved in quality, pricing reflected the upgraded standards.

One of the unspoken risks during Prohibition involved consuming tainted or sometimes lethal brews. Since product grading and evaluating standards were no longer legally employed, alcohol poisoning became a frequent occurrence. Even more dangerous however, was the peril involved in heading a visible criminal gang. The mortality rate at the peak of Prohibition escalated as competition intensified.

Historians have designated Gregorio Conti as Pittsburgh's initial organized crime boss during the 1910s. Stefano

Monastero replaced him. He was more charismatic, cunning and ruthless than his predecessor.

Monastero built a significant local empire structured upon the bones and watered by the blood of his competitors. His fragile network was not built for extended duration nor was his lifespan.

One of his early victims became Luigi Lamendola, widely known as *The Big Gorilla*. At twenty-seven years old, he controlled a moonshine monopoly within the Hill District. He insisted that all neighborhood speakeasy owners purchase their booze from him at inflated prices. Failure to conform would result in beatings, death or having their inventory confiscated. He had direct connections with a crime syndicate in Ontario, Canada for his sourcing. He was rumored to be a former lieutenant of Monastero, but his ambitions vaulted him into the role of unwelcome competitor.

The Big G as associates dared call him rarely strayed from the neighborhood where he maintained a restaurant and furnished apartment upstairs. Lamendola was well aware of the danger he courted competing with Monastero. When he did leave his premises, he traveled heavily armed and carried a cane with a concealed blade of fifteen inches.

On the late evening of May 19, 1927 after closing and locking up his restaurant, he was relaxing inside with a couple of business associates. A large touring car with curtained windows pulled up in front of the building. Two men exited and tapped on his front window asking Lamendola to join them outside.

As he approached his restaurant window, two additional men from inside the car brandished shotguns from behind the curtains. They blasted Lamendola repeatedly shattering glass in stray directions. *The Big Gorilla* expired from eight head wounds. One of his companions was injured from the flying shrapnel. As the vehicle sped away, the gunmen fired repeatedly into Charles Sparano's still operating *New Italian Café* on Chatham at the corner of Webster Street. They narrowly missed the head of a performing violinist from the café orchestra.

Police later traced the vehicle's escape route. They discovered a purposely discarded shotgun on Bigelow Boulevard. A rumor circulated that Lamendola had been murdered with his own shotgun by a member of his gang.

Stefano Monastero may have eliminated one rival, but a more dangerous competitor was Hill District racketeer Joe Pangallo. On September 19, 1927, Pangallo was nearly blown apart when a bomb destroyed his car. He survived the blast and three additional shooting attempts on his life. He earned the moniker the *Ghost of the Hill* for his proficiency in escaping death. Monastero would eternally regret not finishing off Pangallo.

On August 6th, Stefano Monastero and his brother Sam, known as the *Corn Sugar Baron* were visiting a sick friend at Saint John's Hospital in Brighton Heights. The brothers arrived at the hospital in a large steel armored car, with three-quarter-inch thick bulletproof glass. Trailing behind was another armed vehicle that always accompanied them during their four-year reign.

Their precautions proved insufficient for a rival seeking blood revenge.

The brothers exited their vehicle and headed towards the hospital entrance. Five men inside a parked sedan nearby had anticipated their arrival. Each was armed with a sawed off shotgun. The weapons were thrust through the sedan's curtained windows. When the brothers walked into their view, they fired repeatedly.

Stefano dropped immediately from the outgoing fusillade. One of the gunmen would approach his body as he lay expiring in agony. Absent of mercy or pity, the shooter fired several cartridges into his skull at close range.

Sam Monastero fled through the hospital ward and escaped briefly through a rear door. He had been struck during the shooting and left a trail of blood for investigating officers to follow. Monastero would be discovered a block away and detained by police.

Homicide detectives quickly traced the murder to Joe *The Ghost* Pangallo arresting him at his home in McKees Rocks. Pangallo didn't anticipate his sudden capture. He didn't have the time or opportunity to resist arrest with his arsenal of three revolvers and cache of knives and stilettos.

The Ghost had previously evaded violent death. His ultimate end would become more banal and anticlimactic. He died from pneumonia in 1930 never having attained his sought after mob leadership role.

Sam Monastero partially recovered from his wounds and resumed his leadership of the family business. His tenure was short. On March 18, 1930, his body was discovered in the back seat of his new Buick Club Coupe. The vehicle was parked in nearby Bellevue. Monastero was apparently already dead before the vehicle had come to a halt. He had been garroted with his own necktie. A towel was stuffed inside his mouth.

The era of the Monastero Brothers leadership was abruptly terminated. Neither of the brothers, their killers or victims would reach the age of forty. The Saint John's Hospital facility was razed and its 4.8 acres remains vacant and overgrown awaiting a fresh development that may never transpire.

Heading a bootlegging operation would remain hazardous. Future leaders would suffer similar fates. The levels of violence mirrored the conflict the combatants had experienced overseas. This time the battlefield was within their own domestic neighborhoods.

A Proliferation of Illegal Pittsburgh Speakeasies and Vice
William Penn Hotel Speakeasy:
530 William Penn Place, Pittsburgh
John Duffy's Gambling Casino:
5604 Baum Boulevard, Pittsburgh
Joseph Tito's Brothel and Gambling House:
312 Merrimac Street, Pittsburgh Disorderly House

Pittsburgh became a crucial battleground in the struggle to enforce Prohibition laws. The temperance movement never gained a local foothold. Substantial financial gains enjoyed by local crime families entrenched their control over key political and law enforcement leaders.

The corruption however wasn't simply isolated to a specific slice of society. It permeated throughout. Wealthy and marginalized, law abiding and the criminal class demanded their libations. With the general disregard for risk and legal consequences, the flawed regulations were doomed to failure.

Amidst the aristocracy of Pittsburgh, the William Penn Hotel became a favored clandestine destination. The basement bar was renowned for its opulent speakeasy and cautious clientele screening. The hotel was financed by local industrialist Henry Clay Frick and completed in March 1916, shortly before America's entry into World War I.

Frick envisioned the Art Deco aesthetics and opulence to rival the great palaces and hotels of the European continent. Upon completion, the William Penn Hotel became the second tallest property in the world. The hotel has maintained its elevated standards throughout the succeeding century. The illicit gathering salon is currently promoted in the contemporary as the *Speakeasy*.

The space was employed as storage for decades following Prohibition. As novelty destination once again became fashionable, it has been re-christened into a *sophisticated social lounge*. The décor is described as *classic elegance* with *prohibition discretion. Dark and sensual, cozy and private.*

On a very different extremity of the social register, Joseph Tito was arrested on October 23, 1931. He was charged with keeping a disorderly house, code description for brothel. The police found a six and a half gallon moonshine container. Tito would be fined $50 by a magistrate. No account was published regarding the fate of his evening employees.

Police raids became commonplace in residential, commercial and industrial warehouse locations. Competitors furnished many of the tipped-off sites to authorities. One of the largest confiscations occurred on the early morning hours of May 8, 1927. National attention was riveted on the news about a young mail carrier named Charles Lindbergh. He was awaiting favorable weather conditions to conduct his perilous and unprecedented non-stop flight to Paris.

The Baum Boulevard bust netted a substantial liquor inventory, large roulette wheel, birdcage dice game and additional illicit machinery. Attendees and participants were described as *dressed in fashionable evening clothes.* Proprietor John Duffy, nicknamed the *Wheeling Kid* was arrested along with two other operators. Duffy learned marginally from the experience. Five years later he would be convicted of tax evasion for his suspected proceeds earned during 1929. He had reportedly earned $250,000 that year and paid no taxes.

Curbing gambling and drinking within Pittsburgh became a formidable task. The majority of residents across social classes clearly didn't support the concept.

A Nine-Word Presidential Speech of Arid Wit
Carnegie Music Hall
4400 Forbes Avenue, Pittsburgh

On October 13, 1927 President Calvin Coolidge was the invited guest speaker to the Carnegie Institute's 31st Founders Day ceremony. The event was staged at Carnegie Music Hall. Earlier, the Institute's President Samuel Church had extracted a promise from Coolidge to make a *brief* speech of only nine words.

Coolidge was the proper individual to make such a request of. He appeared before the Carnegie Tech student assemblage and spoke: *I shall not break Colonel Church's promise to you.*

He then sat down to thunderous applause.

Calvin Coolidge probably had little aspiration to becoming President of the United States. Born in Vermont, he gradually climbed the political ladder in Massachusetts and was eventually elected governor. He was Warren Harding's *safe* running mate when he ran for the presidency in 1920. The Republican Party was certain they had his unwavering support towards Harding's agenda. Harding was elected handily and then died abruptly under questionable circumstances in 1923. Coolidge became the 30th president.

Coolidge habitually spoke very little and his dry sense of humor often eluded understanding. He was nicknamed *Silent Cal*. He was the first American president to employ the radio in his communications. One can only imagine his adverse reaction towards the intrusion and communication expectations introduced by the Internet. When he died in 1933 five years after leaving office, humorist Dorothy Parker quipped: *How can you tell?*

Following the expiration of Harding's four-year term, Coolidge ran for re-election successfully. He refused to run for a subsequent term. His administration was credited with furthering the women's suffrage movement and he signed into law the Indian Citizenship Act of 1924. He oversaw a booming American economy but his policies of non-intervention and total deregulation of business are cited as an important cause for the 1929 stock market crash and resulting Great Depression.

A Gas Explosion Site Repurposed
Heinz Field:
100 Art Rooney Avenue, Pittsburgh
Carnegie Science Center
1 Allegheny Avenue, Pittsburgh

On November 14, 1927, the largest cylindrical gasometer in the world (at that time) developed a leak. Operated by Equitable Gas on the North Side riverfront of Pittsburgh, the tanks cumulatively contained 5 million cubic feet of natural gas.

Repairmen were summoned to investigate and repair the leak. Several were armed with acetylene torches. They arrived and began inspecting the damage. Presumably some of their torches were ignited.

Abruptly without warning, a loud explosion was followed by three gasometers at the site detonating. A dense mass of smoke and dust preceded an enormous ball of flame estimated at 100 feet in diameter. The fireball expanded to 1,000 feet in height.

The enormity of the explosion damaged the majority of buildings and windows located within a mile radius. Pittsburgh's towering downtown skyscrapers swayed as though impacted by an earthquake.

Over 500 victims would report injuries and 28 individuals would die in the aftermath. The North Side riverside staggered in ruin.

Over the next seventy-five years, the site of the Equitable Gas explosion became long forgotten in local history. More pragmatic concerns and interests superseded. Local professional and college sports teams required a venue to entertain their clientele. The North Side offered available commercial real estate.

Three Rivers Stadium would open in 1970 hosting both the Pirates and Steelers. The stadium would be demolished thirty years later. Heinz Field broke ground in 1999 and open in 2001 to accommodate exclusive football use by the Pittsburgh Steelers and University of Pittsburgh Panthers. It would also be employed for various outdoor entertainment and commercial uses. Adjacent to Heinz Field is the popular Carnegie Science Center.

Both venues are situated at the epicenter of the tragic 1927 Equitable Gas explosion.

Pittsburgh's First Airport and a Tragic Ballooning Disaster
Bettis Airfield:
814 McKeesport Blvd, West Mifflin

Bettis Field is considered Pittsburgh's initial airport established in 1924. Prior to its opening, barnstorming aviators would land on open spaces hoping to evade hidden tree stumps and other potential obstacles.

The airstrip was originally known as the Pittsburgh-McKeesport Airport. The composition was essentially a 144-acre property featuring grassy stretches of meadow and pasture. Landowner Harry Neel and a small group local investors created the commercial flying field.

Crowds assembled on the weekends to view wing aerobatics and take sightseeing excursions. During its initial year, the savage growth became graded. Aviation fuel and oil were sold to pilots. In 1925, the field became a base of operations for airmail service under government contract. The U.S. Army began landing transports, bombers and pursuit planes. Parachute jumping and air races followed.

That same year, the ceremony opening the field to the public was presided over by Lieutenant Cyrus Bettis of the U.S. Army Corps.

One year later, the airport would be renamed after Bettis who then owned the current world flying speed record of 249 mph. In 1926, Bettis was leading a formation of three Army airplanes when they encountered heavy fog. His plane struck several treetops and crashed into Jack's Mountain near Bellefonte.

Bettis survived the impact and crawled injured to a road several miles away. He was rescued and admitted to Walter

Reed Hospital. Seemingly on the mend from his wounds, he died fourteen days later suddenly from complications.

In 1927, aviator Charles Lindbergh landed at Bettis Field in his plane the *Spirit of St. Louis* during his global goodwill tour. He was feted by a Pittsburgh parade while his plane was hangered sideways per his explicit instructions. He departed from the airfield the following day at noon.

On May 31, 1928, the National Elimination Hot Air Balloon Races were staged at Bettis Field witnessed by an estimated 150,000 spectators. Despite adverse weather forecasts, fourteen entrants lifted off at 6:00 a.m.

Within a half hour, the balloons were trapped in a horrendous thunderstorm. Several were hit by direct lightening strikes. U.S. Army Balloon #3 was struck near Youngwood. The pilot, Lieutenant Paul Evert was electrocuted immediately. His balloon caught fire at 1,200 feet. His sole passenger, Lieutenant Uzal Ent was able to safely land the burning aircraft on private property.

The balloon collapsed approximately twenty feet above the ground. The depleting hydrogen gas would set fire and destroy the envelope and net. Evert would be buried in the Arlington National Cemetery. Another balloonist, W.W. Morton was also listed as a fatality from the same event.

By 1929, Bettis Field had become a financial casualty of the growing Depression. The novelty of viewing recreational stunt planes and barnstormers was wearing off. Two years later, the nearby larger and modern Allegheny County Airport would open. The facility absorbed military, governmental and commercial uses and contracts. Bettis Field ownership would change subsequently on several occasions.

The airfield would eventually evolve into a military training facility during World War II. It was sold to Westinghouse in January 1949. The property would be redeveloped becoming the Bettis Atomic Power Laboratory. Its two paved runways were used for parking. The Art Deco styled terminal building was discreetly razed during the 2000s leaving scant memory of its once prominent history. Admission to the public is currently prohibited.

A Female Aviator Clipped By The Social Mores of Her Era
Employer: Pittsburgh Golf Club *(Formerly Pittsburgh Country Club)*
5280 Northumberland Street, Pittsburgh

Rose Collins never achieved the renown of fellow female aviation pioneer Amelia Earhart. Collins was acknowledged as the first woman granted an aviator's license application in Pennsylvania in 1929.

Collins was taught to fly at the Morris Flying School at Rogers Air Field in O'Hara. Her instructor was Captain William J. Austin, a former World War I pilot. As a military aviator, Austin became one of the first recognized 400 fliers.

At the age of 25, simply enrolling as a flying student elevated Collins into local recognition. She was spotlighted in a January 21, 1929 Gimbels Department Store advertising spread. Her full-page photo posing beside a plane at Rodgers Field proudly proclaimed that Gimbels had outfitted her. The caption appearing below indicted that she already accumulated a considerable number of flying hours and *is about ready to solo*.

Rose Collins was potentially soon to be known on a much grander scale. Her necessary licensing solo flight, however, would never materialize.

Sketchy details are known about Collin's past. She was born in impoverished Connellsville in 1904 to an extensive family of thirteen. Only seven children would survive to adulthood. At 15, Rose reportedly worked as a department store clerk in Beaver Creek. She moved to Pittsburgh and began employment as a secretary between 1926-29 at the Pittsburgh Country Club.

She never expressed what was her inspiration to become a pilot. One may easily presume that her primary influence was the fame and worldwide exposure of Amelia Earhart.

Earhart's storied aviation career and mysterious flight disappearance in 1937 remains a twentieth century enigma. She was an intelligent, articulate and charismatic personality. She was ideally suited to become a serious and admired icon.

Her own direct association with Pittsburgh became two visits during the summer of 1928. In July, she passed through the city briefly following her becoming the first woman to cross the Atlantic Ocean via airplane. On that voyage, she was relegated to passenger, not pilot. She was greeted by an admiring local population and interviewed by the local press on her views regarding the future of flight.

On August 31, 1928, she would return under inglorious conditions. Earhart crash landed her plane onto Rodgers Field after misjudging the necessary landing distance on the grass runway. It is possible that an ambitious Rose Collins may have encountered her on one of her visits.

Earhart would make the first female solo trans-Atlantic flight in 1932 between Newfoundland and Derry, Northern Ireland. Three years later, she became the first aviator to fly solo from Honolulu to Oakland, California. Her accomplishments, ambition and daring exploits astonished caustic observers. Her feminist advocacy inspired women.

Following her January 1929 newspaper exposure, Rose Collins was photographed again on February 25th preparing to spin the propeller for the first biplane that had arrived for the Pittsburgh Aircraft Show. The event was scheduled for March 9-16 at the Motor Square Garden in East Liberty.

The Aero Club of Pittsburgh sponsored this initial event that featured 100 exhibits and 23 airplanes. Collins was linked by the press into promotional announcements and acknowledged as inviting Mayor Charles Kline to the event's Aero Club Ball. She was frequently acknowledged as Pittsburgh's impending first female aviator.

She was subsequently featured in a local newspaper profile identifying international female pilots entitled *Women Take to the Air*. Her exposure was expanding.

Her next major exposure in the May 14th edition was a photo of her seated inside an airplane. Her death notice accompanied the photo.

The timing and shock behind the announcement was worsened by her printed cause of death. Her demise was listed as following the aftermath *of an operation performed by a woman*. Collins had died the day before at Passavant Hospital in the Hill District. She had refused to name the woman who performed the operation before she expired. Her death certificate cited *peritonitis*.

Anyone reading the understood meaning knew that it was from a botched abortion.

Six weeks later, the father was revealed as Sergeant Leo Herman, chief clerk of the Rodgers Field air corps. He identified himself as Collin's fiancé and claimed that *he had urged her to marry him and not undergo the surgery*.

It was an alternative that didn't appeal to Rose Collins.

She had emerged from the poverty of her coal-mining hometown and was on the cusp of ascending to her potential dreams. An unwanted husband and child were not part of the trajectory. Unstable local weather and pregnancy morning sickness likely were the causes for her delayed solo flight. She had already attained the necessary preliminary flight hours.

Rose Collins' name may have ultimately extended beyond. She was young, attractive and buoyant. The cultural restraints imposed upon an unwed mother or tethered wife then prompted her into a drastic and ultimately fatal decision. The desire for fame frequently has adverse consequences. Her abortionist was never identified.

On July 1, 1929, Helen Richey of McKeesport would become the first female to officially qualify as a pilot in Allegheny County.

1929
HELEN RICHEY

**Pittsburgh's Vanished Icons From the 1930-1950s Jazz
Era
The Bachelor's Club Former Site:
6308 Penn Avenue, Pittsburgh
Liberty Avenue Musicians Sculpture:
947 Liberty Avenue, Pittsburgh
Crawford Grill:
2141 Wylie Avenue, Pittsburgh**

The Jazz Age proliferated within Pittsburgh for three decades beginning in the 1930s. The most popular clubs were concentrated in the downtown, Hill and East Liberty districts. Despite the restrictions and limitations imposed by segregation, black performers were in peak demand. Their fame had pronounced boundaries. The majority of musicians were consigned to lodging in rooming houses or cheap motels within the Hill District.

The more prosperous and renowned acts such as the Duke Ellington orchestra would arrive by rail in their own Pullman cars at Pennsylvania Union Station. Following their sold-out performances, the band would simply transfer the festivities, impromptu jam sessions and sleeping arrangements to their Pullmans at the station.

The composition of jazz venue audiences were frequently desegregated and a lethal cocktail of celebrities, politicians, gangsters, sportsmen and jazz devotees.

Downtown featured clubs, casinos, burlesque houses and strip joints. Revelers could drift from venue to venue. Speakeasies were plentiful during Prohibition. Among the most reputed and notorious landing spots were the Variety Club, Chelsea, Almono and the Benjamin Harrison Literary Club.

The Harrison Literary Club had zero academic pretensions. It was a serious drinking magnet to visit and be seen. It attracted controversy and periodically scandal.

A local political fixer named John J. Verona went club hopping on the late evening of January 11, 1937. He completed his rounds during the early morning hours at the Harrison Literary Club. He loudly serenaded his companions in song with his noteworthy baritone voice inside a dimly lit back room.

Verona was stoutly built with a ravenous appetite for spirited living and dining. His singing left him famished. He approached the club bar to order a sandwich. Another patron took the opportunity to insult him. Verona had once been a diehard Republican. He'd altered his political alignment to support Democratic President Franklin Roosevelt. His bar tormentor called him a *turncoat*.

Verona resented the remark. His response was to exchange heated words and ultimately blows. One of Verona's companions knocked the offending man unconscious. A melee followed. Verona abruptly collapsed to the floor.

Verona, 44, died from a massive heart attack. The brawl concluded the legacy of a political influencer from the Hill District. The printed media accounts minimized the significance of the fight contributing to his death.

Three days afterwards, Verona's funeral drew an overflowing crowd estimated at 10,000. Mourners packed St. Peter's Church and the fronting on Fernando Street. The Harrison Club would later be renamed the Southern Outing and Fishing Club. Little changed. The atmosphere was volatile with excessive boozing, hooking up and premium entertainment.

Locally born talent Maxine Sullivan began as a waitress at the club until she started singing in her uncle's band *The Red Hot Peppers*. She would perform at the Southern Outing regularly before establishing a distinctive international half-century career.

On Pittsburgh's East End, venues such as Lepus, Del Mar Canoe Club and the Bachelors Club booked impressive talent. Prominent future stars performing early career gigs including Jerry Lewis, Dean Martin, Lenny Bruce, Gypsy Rose Lee, Ella Fitzgerald and Vic Damone.

A surprise state police raid on the Bachelors Club in April 1941 resulted in 129 persons being detained, a third of them women. The club had no liquor license. An extensive inventory of choice spirits and gambling paraphernalia were confiscated. The officers conducting the raid required 15 minutes of intense sledgehammer pounding to crash through six steel doors fortifying the club entrance.

The Bachelors Club location has since become a residential apartment complex within the high-tech oriented Bakery Square development.

Remembrance of Pittsburgh's jazz era is tragically marginal.

James Simon's three 15-foot sculptures entitled *Liberty Avenue Musicians* located on the same street offers visual homage. The currently designated Cultural and Historic District formally flourished as a popular musical destination.

One of the most prominent outlets was the Black Musicians Club featuring playing gigs for traveling musicians.

Jazz icons such as Dizzy Gillespie, Jimmy Heath, Ben Webster and Coleman Hawkins played there. Other featured acts showcased throughout Pittsburg included Art Tatum, Nat

King Cole, Erroll Garner, Jimmie Lunceford, Bennie Moten and Cab Calloway, a veritable *Who's Who* of jazz royalty.

Besides the Black Musicians Club, other premium headliner venues included the Copa, Hurricane and Crawford Grills. The Hill District featured the Ritz, Showboat, Roosevelt Theatre, Savoy Ballroom, Loendi and Washington Club. Northside was Red's Club, Pace's and the Moose.

The remaining Crawford Grill edifice staggers as a lone testament to the former vitality and prestige of the Hill district. The monolith lurches singularly and in evident decline. The majority of neighborhood structures have been razed with evidence of reconstruction planned in the future. That future will never replicate again the former vigor of the jazz era.

Fresher musical movements have eclipsed the popularity and significance of jazz. These musical reincarnations have cannibalized their influences. What was once considered *contemporary* is simply relegated to *old school*. Knowledgeable purists know better than to accept this fallacy.

A Gruesome Murder of A Double-Crossing Booze Runner
William Gregory's Former Address: 1234 Sheffield Street,
Pittsburgh
Philip De Fazio's Wildcat Brewery: 4740 Lorigan Street,
Pittsburgh

At the pinnacle of Pittsburgh's bootlegging purge, local press accounts sensationalized readers with explicit reporting. None exceeded the grotesque elaboration detailing the death of twenty-three-year old booze runner William Gregory.

Gregory became intoxicated by the prospect of skimming revenue from his employers. During March 1930, he was assigned by a Pittsburgh crime syndicate to make a beer delivery to a Pennsylvania-based client near the Ohio border. He'd worked with this syndicate for only six weeks. Gregory left with a beer shipment from a Lorigan Street residential brewery. He convinced a friend to follow him in his automobile.

Instead of simply completing the delivery, Gregory continued to Akron, Ohio. He sold the truck to a used car dealer for $400 and the beer consignment to a private party. The vehicle had been registered in his name, but belonged to Philip De Fazio, the syndicate's leader.

Gregory kept the entire proceeds and returned to Pittsburgh foolishly certain that he could explain the disappearance of both vehicle and contents.

Two weeks prior, he made arrangements for his wife and two children to remain in Akron. It was speculated that he might have intended to reunite with them now flush with cash.

Gregory understood the risk he was courting. He expressed his fears of retribution to friends upon returning to Pittsburgh. These concerns proved justified.

Gregory was a gambler and an unconvincing liar. He fabricated two contradictory accounts. He related to acquaintances that he'd been hijacked near the state line. To De Fazio and syndicate members, he explained that Federal Prohibition agents had seized both the truck and beer shipment. When confronted by the conflicting versions, he was unable to satisfy the syndicate.

Philip De Fazio didn't hesitate with his vengeance for the evident double-cross. On March 31, 1930, Gregory returned to an empty Lorigan Street brewery where De Fazio normally stored his shipment inventory. Gregory's was probably struck in the back of his head by a wrench and then tortured repeatedly. His mutilated and decapitated body was stuffed into a cabbage barrel. The discarded barrel would be discovered days later shrouded in the nearby countryside.

The savagery of the attack was so vicious that even with the walls and floors being scrubbed with lime, bloodstains remained visible. Police arrested De Fazio afterwards based on the implication of Gregory's friend Helen Lightner and his step-father-in-law. Lightner indicated that she'd last seen Gregory on the day of his death. He was heading for work at the brewery preparing to advise De Fazio on the details regarding the missing shipment. The step-father-in-law confirmed De Fazio owned the truck.

A seemingly straightforward case of a revenge murder on a double-crossing victim became murkier. Shortly after Gregory's murder, Helen Lightner and her husband with one of his friends were captured leaving Pittsburgh in Gregory's automobile.

Gregory's wife and children could not be located in Akron. There were published fears that his killers had abducted them.

Deeper investigation revealed that Lightner had originally met Gregory in January 1930 when both resided in the same rooming house. They engaged in an extra-marital affair. Gregory was portrayed as a serial womanizer particularly during his delivery runs. He frequently abandoned his wife and children for sporadic lengths of time.

Could a jealous cuckolded husband or lover have instead perpetrated his murder?

On April 8th, Gregory's wife and children were reportedly located in an Akron suburb. She was unaware of her husband's death and agreed to return to Pittsburgh to identify the body.

Local newspaper accounts had convincingly convicted Philip De Fazio of murder before his trial. Another beer runner, James Moleno came forward indicating that De Fazio had contacted him with the intention of ordering Gregory's murder.

With extreme media bias, the murder trial of Philip De Fazio was initiated in early June. The prosecution sought the death penalty. The defense argued the *real culprit had fled the jurisdiction of the court directly after the crime.*

The prosecution did not introduce the bloodstained wrench into evidence. There was never confirmed indication as to whether the blood was Gregory's. Much of their case was presumably constructed on circumstantial and hearsay evidence. On June 13th, the jury voted to acquit De Fazio of murder charges.

In the aftermath, two witnesses from the trial were arrested for liquor distribution charges based on testimony they gave on behalf of De Fazio. The accused had testified during the trial that he had paid Allegheny county politicians $350,000 in protection monies over seven years to operate his bootlegging business.

DeFazio was freed from Gregory's murder charge, but now targeted by the district attorney on much wider ranging charges of graft and corruption. On June 18th, De Fazio went missing. He was last sighted wearing a red sweater and boarding White Star Bus Lines service to Wheeling, West Virginia.

His wife, Rose Cocthini was reportedly raised in Wheeling. Investigators visited all of the De Fazio families within the city. None would claim to have any relatives living within the United States. The code of silence shielded Philip DeFazio from identification or his whereabouts. Existing state extradition laws prevented the further expansion of the investigation.

Philip De Fazio would never be heard from in Pittsburgh again.

A Grocery Store Massacre Stimulating More Questions Than Answers
Former Lobianco Brothers Grocery Store Location:
419 Sixth Street, Braddock

One of the most shocking killings during an era of blood frenzy occurred on Saturday morning, October 4, 1930. The victims initially appeared disconnected from any mob related activities.

Shortly after 9:00 a.m., owners Carmen and Joseph Lobianco were stocking inventory shelves inside their Lobianco Brothers grocery store in Braddock. A lone gunman walked into the store and shot the brothers to death along with Joseph's pregnant wife Mary. Doctors could not save her unborn child.

The seemingly senseless killing became further clouded when investigators discovered that the store's inventory was almost exclusively sugar and yeast. Days later, cancelled checks were discovered that had been endorsed by gangster James Volpe. When questioned by police, Volpe claimed the checks were repayment for loans.

Investigators accepted his questionable explanation. The killer of the foursome would never be discovered. The location site has since become integrated into the Braddock Police Department headquarters building.

**Straddling A Delicate Balancing Risk With Law
Enforcement and Bootleggers
Morris Curran's Bombed Business:
1233-35 Penn Avenue, Pittsburgh
Morris Curran's Murder Site:
2922 Perryville Avenue, Pittsburgh**

Three days before the shooting death of mobster Stefano Monastero, rival Morris Curran received a surprise of his own. Explosives blew out the facade of his brick retail establishment. His reported lost inventory was itemized in the newspaper as copper coils and tanks, kegs, corks, bottles, funnels, bottling machines and corn sugar. Each of these materials was integral in producing illegal moonshine.

In the *Pittsburgh Post-Gazette* profile of the bomb blast, Curran boasted that he was a *progressive man* and blamed *professional jealousy* as the motive behind the destruction. He shrugged off the moonshine coincidence explaining that *he wasn't interested in what his customers do with their purchases-all he did was sell it to them.*

In the same article Curran refused to admit that he was a bootlegger and vowed to continue his supply business *until he made enough to quit.*

Two female neighbors were injured from the blast. They were hurled from their residential beds and showered with broken glass. There were no fatalities.

The bombing would later be attributed to Curran's refusal to join an association of bootlegging suppliers. Their intention was to equally distribute the commerce amongst members preventing underpricing. Curran rationalized that the volume of his current trade was entrenched without their assistance. The bombing failed to spook him into quitting.

For nearly two years following the explosion, Curran indeed continued his bootlegging supply business. His competitors despised him. He played a dangerous intrigue of double crossing his customers. His goal was to become an indispensable conduit, the *dictator* of the citywide bootlegging industry.

Curran betrayed his customers by duplicating their invoice slips for brewing still equipment purchases. He would give them a copy and then provide prohibition agents with a second. Days later, agents would conduct raids on his client's premises destroying their production capability and confiscating their inventory.

Curran then visited the damaged facilities sharing his condolences with distraught owners for their loss. He simultaneously offered to outfit the facility once again or at a fresh location of their choosing. The cycle would continue again with a subsequent police raid.

Eventually his duplicity became recognized. No one welcomed a snitch especially amongst criminals. His role as informer made him vulnerable and immediately disposable.

On June 24, 1931, he was gunned down on the sidewalk as he strolled out of his newly constructed residence. The news coverage outed him as a *stool pigeon*.

The man who'd determined to rise to dictator status by straddling a dangerous balance was now reviled as simply another gangland casualty. His killer(s) would never be identified.

A Devastating Fire Affecting the City's Most Vulnerable Population
Former Site of Little Sisters of the Poor: Penn Avenue at S. Aiken Avenue, Pittsburgh
Saint Paul Cathedral: 108 N Dithridge Street, Pittsburgh

1931 was grim throughout Pittsburgh. The Great Depression was barely past its first year and the impoverished were already feeling the financial pinch. Unemployment was skyrocketing, hunger was devastating families and the needs of the elderly were generally ignored. Precedent certainties appeared irrelevant when simply surviving through another day became a grinding challenge.

On July 24, 1931, a fire that erupted inside the Little Sisters of the Poor elderly home in the Lawrenceville district accentuated the collective misery. The source of the blaze was never publicized, but ignited shortly after the resident's bedtime. Neighbors who sounded an alarm sighted the flames. Fireman and police would be summoned by six subsequent alarms in rapid succession.

A reported 250-300 individuals resided within the facility. Many were infirmed and all were aged. Firemen were able to rescue many from the four-story building and several leapt into life nets from the upper story windows.

The catastrophe could have been far worse as the flames spread throughout the facility. The institution's Mother Superior was instrumental in assisting numerous residents to escape from the building. She finally had to be forcibly detained from entering when conditions were at the peak of danger. An estimated 20,000 spectators would linger to view the inferno.

Ambulances, taxis and privately owned cars transported more than 100 victims to various hospitals within Pittsburgh. The hastily coordinated effort preserved lives. Forty-seven people would ultimately die. The blaze was contained by 11:30 p.m., but the building was destroyed beyond redemption.

Family, friends or relatives took the majority of the dead away for burial. Eight unclaimed victims remained inside the morgue. Their bodies were transferred to Saint Paul Cathedral where Bishop Hugh Boyle presided over a funeral mass for them. Local residents of all denominations filled the pews for the August 3rd mass. They collected an offering that paid for burial caskets for the deceased.

The grief from the fire had briefly unified a community splintered by financial hard times. The trials from the Depression would worsen. The residential site today serves as the grounds for the Children's Home of Pittsburgh and Lemieux Family Center. Their operations serve another fragile element of the community.

The Yeast Baron is Silenced Amidst Gangster Turf Wars
Empire Yeast Company Site:
241 Cedarville Street, Pittsburgh
Giuseppe Siragusa Murder Site:
2523 Beechwood Boulevard, Pittsburgh

During the Prohibition era, being *put on the spot* was the vernacular for being murdered by a contract killer. Joseph Siragusa had ascended to prominence as the *Yeast Baron* within the bootlegger trade. His Empire Yeast Company reportedly handled nearly a ton of yeast everyday to predominantly six clients.

Siragusa created a distribution combine to regulate the price of yeast locally. The group met several times during the week inside his offices. Their objective was to maintain pricing at nearly their acquired levels to freeze out smaller retail competition.

As competitors dropped out of the business unable to match the combine's pricing levels, a monopoly was created. Siragusa's combine would later raise prices to compensate having effectively eliminated competition.

As an outsider peering in, one of Siragusa's former rivals decided to form his own combine. His project required the removal of Siragusa. He recruited a New York hit man to put Siragusa *on the spot*.

Despite his growing affluence and acclaim, Siragusa was vulnerable. He employed no bodyguards for protection. He and his wife Mary lived in a spacious Squirrel Hill neighborhood residence. On September 13, 1931, his wife returned with her mother from church services. Siragusa was found sprawled on his basement steps dead. He had been shot in the face, chest and arm.

Joseph Gallo, 32, emerged as a suspect two weeks later when his New York license plates were identified on a parked sedan by neighbors. The vehicle was presumed to be the killer's. Witnesses were unable to identify Gallo as either driver or passenger. Police reasoned that a contract killer would never display his personal out-of-state plates on a vehicle. Gallo was released. Additional suspects would never materialize.

Cleaning House By Eliminating Two Pittsburgh Chieftains
Jack Palmere Murder Site:
Pittsburgh Marriot City Center
112 Washington Place, Pittsburgh (Formerly 700 Block of Wylie)
Jack Palmere Residence:
2022 Pioneer Avenue, Pittsburgh

Jack Palmere, 35, had repeated a dangerous selling strategy that had cost peers Morris Curran and Giuseppe Siragusa their lives. Within their clientele base, each had strategically underpriced their competition.

Palmere had evolved into a conspicuous local presence. He drove a pretentious car and dressed immaculately. He knew that he had been targeted to become the one hundred and second racketeering related casualty within the past six years. The realization that his death might be only hours away petrified him as he made his rounds.

On the evening of October 7, 1931, Palmere pulled his car up to the curb in the 700 block of Wylie Avenue shorting after 7 p.m. He exited his vehicle and began conversing with an acquaintance, Fred Colelli, on the sidewalk. He confided to him the dangerous predicament that ensnared him.

While in conversation facing Colelli, a stocky man strode around the corner from Chatham Street pacing rapidly towards the pair. The man casually pulled out a revolver and fired repeatedly into Palmere leaving him sprawled in the gutter.

Palmere died instantly. Witnesses saw the gunman flee and enter a house on Wylie Avenue. A police search of the residence produced no clues. By the following day, investigators were certain they knew who was the killer. He would be identified as *Little Joe* Spinelli, a New York based hitman.

Within 18 hours following Palmere's murder, Spinelli violently liquidated another target, Saverio *Toto* Amaraso. His intended victim had been on the run for several days knowing that his legacy was nearly certain to become short-lived. Amaraso had attempted to evade his potential assassin by sleeping with his clothes on and never remaining in the same overnight location consecutively.

He heard the news of Palmere's death probably from Spinelli himself, as he'd been a former bodyguard for both men.

Spinelli knew where to locate *Toto* Amaraso. He knocked on the front door of a Church Avenue building at 8:00 a.m. on October 8th. The building, since renumbered or leveled was the location for one of Amaraso's stills.

Inside, Amaraso was pacing the third floor. He'd ordered two associates to admit no one so that he might sleep. Repose proved elusive and his eyes were rimmed with red. He likely presumed Spinelli could be trusted. He left the building with him for an appointment with death.

Spinelli drove him three miles from the Turtle Creek neighborhood to a trickling creek located off Hall Station Road, a half mile from Linhart. Amaraso would be strangled, wrapped in a blanket soaked with gasoline and then torched.

Police investigators stormed the Church Avenue building later in the morning, but too late. Amaraso's associates identified Spinelli as Amaraso's escort out. Police discovered Amaraso's flaming body shortly before noon. Spinelli had vanished and reportedly would never be apprehended.

New York criminal interests made Pittsburgh a desirable marketplace. Eliminating the entrenched local hierarchy became imperative for their entrance. The thinning process remained nearly complete.

**Father James Cox: Action Not Rhetoric
St. Patrick's Church:
1711 Liberty Avenue, Pittsburgh**

James Renshaw Cox proved himself a man of the people more exemplary than any political figure. He was born on March 7, 1886 in Lawrenceville. Never shying away from toil, he worked during his formative years as a newsboy, department store clerk, mill hand, railroad worker and taxicab agent.

Between his employments, he studied at the Holy Ghost College (currently Duquesne University) and earned his bachelor's degree. He continued his education at the seminary at St. Vincent's in Latrobe and was ordained on July 11, 1911 at the age of twenty-five.

Father Cox determined early that he would never become a pedestrian priest. In 1917 during World War I, he traveled to France to serve two years at a hospital. When he returned to Pittsburgh, he became the designated chaplain of Mercy Hospital. He continued his studies and earned a master's degree in education from the University of Pittsburgh. The distinction made him the first Catholic priest to earn a degree there.

In 1923, he was appointed the pastor of the city's oldest house of worship, St. Patrick's Church. Not surprisingly, the ambitious Cox was the youngest ever named to that position.

Father Cox ascended to his pastoral title when the medium of radio was first introduced. Although soon becoming a Pittsburgh institution, his weekly broadcasts expanded his audience throughout Western Pennsylvania.

His greatest virtue was commitment to the homeless and unemployed population that had been expanding significantly despite a boom economy. He established a soup kitchen in 1925 and was a visible personality in the shantytowns that accumulated near his church and the Strip District. As the subsequent Great Depression ravaged the community, he lobbied local merchants and businessmen to donate liberally towards the less fortunate. He ceaselessly fundraised for relief organizations and was nicknamed the *Shepherd of the Unemployed*.

Father Cox was overwhelmed by the immensity of the problem and growing unrest. He decided to organize a march to Washington D.C. that he actively promoted through his radio broadcasts and diocese.

On January 5, 1932, an estimated 45,000 people gathered to march to Washington. He organized convoys of trucks and cars to transport participants. Pittsburgh native and Treasury Secretary Andrew Mellon authorized his Gulf Oil gas stations to dispense complimentary gasoline to participating vehicles. President Herbert Hoover prompted Mellon to resign when he found out. The scale of the Depression dominated Hoover's presidency and permanently tarnished his legacy and reputation.

Father Cox was always clear on his objectives and insisted of his followers to not carry alcohol, weapons or engage in chronic complaining.

The aftermath of the march created a political organization called the Jobless Party. Their platform supported governmental public works and labor unions. They stressed that these public programs were a tangible alternative to the nation lapsing into communism. Father Cox became the party's initial presidential candidate. He dropped out of the race in September 1932 to support Democratic candidate Franklin Roosevelt. His withdrawal ended the Jobless Party. He was more effective as a priest than a fledging politician.

Old St. Patrick's Church would be destroyed by fire on March 21, 1935. A more diminutive replacement structure with the same name would be constructed on the site. It remains today.

One of Father Cox's final ideological confrontations became a forceful denouncement of another radio priest, Detroit based Father Charles E. Coughlin. Since the 1930s, Coughlin had employed his radio platform to blame bankers, labor unions, socialists, communists and internationalists for causing the depression. His most vile attacks were anti-Semitic. Father Cox attacked him directly in a 1939 speech that prompted an accompanying pamphlet. Within a couple of years, Coughlin lost his radio contract and was censored by the Catholic Church.

Father Cox toned down his activities during the 1940s due to declining health and concentrated on his parish responsibilities and commitment to the poor. He died on March 20, 1951 with a meager estate of barely $1,000. Amassing personal wealth was never his objective. His actions epitomized what believers and even agnostics seek in a man committed to God, but rarely discover. His life and example consistently embodied his preaching.

The Violent Fall of the House of Volpe
Frank Manna's Barbershop:
Currently BNY Mellon Client Service Center, 500 Ross
Street, Pittsburgh *(Formerly 527 Fifth Avenue)*
Volpe Murder Site/Formerly Rome Coffee Shop
PPG Paints Arena South Parking Lot *(Formerly 704 Wylie*
Street)

The successive murders of Stefano and Sam Monastero, Morris Curran, Giuseppe Siragusa and Jack Palmere created a leadership void within Pittsburgh's bootlegging trade. Eight brothers composed the criminal Volpe family, the lords of the southeastern suburban Wilmerding.

1932 would become a horrendous year for the family fortunes. Chester Volpe had been killed in a 1931 New Years Eve car wreck on the corner of Penn Avenue and Ninth Street. Louis Volpe was incarcerated inside the Allegheny County Jail for a bootlegging conviction.

The worse news resonated in mid-summer.

On Friday, July 29, 1932, John Volpe, the acknowledged leader entered Frank Manna's barbershop at noon. His daily custom included a shave and shoeshine. On Saturdays, he would receive a haircut and manicure. Following the barber's detailing, he strolled down Wylie Avenue. He passed the site of Jack Palmare's previous year assassination. He stopped briefly inside a nearby drugstore to order a milkshake

He then continued to the Rome Coffee Shop, which served as the brother's Pittsburgh headquarters. Two brothers, James and Arthur awaited him at a small round table in the rear. Arthur was eating a lunch consisting of corn flakes.

John Volpe had earlier parked his distinctive light green 16-

cylinder Cadillac coupe nearby. The custom designed mini-fortress was fortified with bulletproof glass windows.

John checked inside with his brothers exchanging idle conversation. It would be their final words spoken together. He then stepped outside to survey the Wylie Avenue panorama. At approximately 12:45 p.m., a dark blue Ford sedan cruised past and parked next to a curb nearby.

The vehicle's presence fated doom. John recognized the three men exiting dressed in business suits. One was reportedly Giuseppe *Big Mike* Spinelli, a former friend and bodyguard. Each was carrying a pistol and heading towards John Volpe.

Volpe sensed instinctively their intent and attempted to flee towards his parked car. His premonition came too late. He would be gunned down by five shots collapsing on the sidewalk against a woman named Antoinette Ferarro. She fainted. The intended executions weren't complete. The trio entered the coffee shop and sighted the two remaining brothers.

James Volpe bolted to hide behind the steel counter, but was struck by three bullets in the back of the head. One reportedly tore off part of his face. Table and chairs were scattered as the gunmen sought out Arthur. He was located and executed with two shots to the back of the head. The remaining café patrons were spared. The gunmen returned to their sedan and headed east.

A priest from the nearby St. Ann's Catholic Church read John Volpe his last rights. He was likely already deceased. A news photographer from the *Pittsburgh Sun-Telegraph* captured images of the carnage that saturated the afternoon edition's headlines.

Police combed the neighborhood for clues and eyewitnesses.

The sole admitted witness inside the café was Santo Bazzano, a friend of the brother's. He spent the shooting spree cowering behind the counter wailing *I don't wanna be shot. I don't wanna be shot.*

The neighborhood yielded no assistance. Several individuals had heard the shots, but no one claimed to accurately view or describe the shooters. Some claimed they thought it was simply cap pistols. Their avoidance to become involved was understandable. The shooting was clearly a gangland hit and the killers remained at large. Personal involvement might incite revenge.

Incarcerated brother Louis Volpe heard about the news when he read the late-edition newspaper. He reportedly *blanched slightly*, but displayed no overt emotion. He calmly returned to his cell and would later request permission to attend his brothers' funeral.

The prestige of the Volpe name was immediately challenged. The car dealership became anxious to impound the custom coupe. John Volpe still owed them $7,500. It was prudently determined that until the killers were apprehended, the vehicle might remain a target. It was housed temporarily inside a Webster Avenue garage.

Local political personalities such as Pittsburgh Mayor Charles Kline brayed and protested the brazen mid-day murders. Two months earlier, he had been convicted of corruption charges and would be soon facing a year in prison. He and the current police superintendent who face his own corruption indictment claimed the murder was an *affront* and *immediate priority to solve*.

Their public overtures were understandable. The House of Volpe had financially supported both men with lucrative payoffs. The Volpe's ultimate return on investment would become paltry following the shootings.

On the evening of their death, an open casket display for the three brothers was arranged by Wilmerding's Jones Funeral Home (no longer in operation). The morticians were praised for discreetly employing sheets partially concealing the bodies to hide the bullet wounds.

Thousands during the weekend would line up to view the brothers there and inside the family residence. Some wept as they filed past, some bent down to kiss the frigid faces and others knelt in prayer.

The Volpe clan lived a few blocks away from the facility. The women and children reportedly grieved with *uncontrolled sobs, moaning* and *hysterical shrill curses*. Two other brothers remained with their mother *serious but tearless*.

Louis Volpe had been permitted to leave jail for a few hours to briefly visit his family. The crowd around their residence parted as he arrived with a U. S. Marshall escort. Upon viewing the caskets, widows and their children, he burst out crying.

The funeral procession was conducted on Monday, August 1, 1932 without the blessing of the local St. Aloysius Catholic Church. An estimated 250 vehicles fronted the bedlam with over 5,000 in attendance.

Lead gangster John Volpe had attained a mythical sainthood within Wilmerding. Like any perceived Don, his generosity was magnified to excess. One observer noted that for the local children *his death was like having their Santa Claus taken away*.

The police proved impotent in capturing the Volpe killers. Retribution for the crime however was rapidly completed.

Investigators interviewed an unassuming local racketeer John Bazzano at their headquarters. Bazzano had a firm alibi and his own brother Santo had been concealed inside the café during the shooting. Bazzano reiterated his friendship with the Volpe's and the police found no reason to detain him. They did keep his house under surveillance. He effortlessly eluded them for an ordered trip to New York City.

Although the police publicly professed ignorance regarding Volpe's killers, New York City's La Cosa Nostra Commission was certain. The commission was a governing body of crime families that arbitrated internal disputes and lethally punished offenders that had overstepped boundaries.

John Bazzano was immediately summoned before them on August 6th. He dressed to impress the next evening and was feted as the guest of honor inside an abandoned building in the Red Hook section of Brooklyn. Amidst the banquet, he was toasted for orchestrating the Volpe Brothers slaying. He was being set up to lower his guard. Afterwards, he was offered a ride back to his hotel.

Bazzano was unaware that his drivers were loyal to the Volpe's. He never arrived to the hotel. Instead it was speculated that Bazzano was brought before the commission to defend his unsanctioned actions. His excuse apparently was unconvincing.

In the predawn darkness, his body would be discovered tossed inside a large burlap bag near a refuse pile. He had been tied up with rope and gagged with a handkerchief. Mob justice had ordered him stabbed twenty times with an ice pick.

His funeral on Saturday, August 13 was a more sedate and discrete ceremony than the Volpe brothers. A priest had blessed the body inside his home. A procession of 75 cars, seven loaded with flowers, accompanied his widow, brother and mourners to the gravesite for burial.

Days later, fourteen men would be detained by New York City police for involvement with the murder. No one talked and no damning evidence materialized. The group was charged with loitering and released. John Bazzano's murder would remain officially unsolved.

Bazzano's death foreshadowed the demise of Prohibition. The repeal officially became law on April 7, 1933. A reported 50,000 local residents would gather around Pittsburgh's three major breweries awaiting their first legal sip and purchase since thirteen years before.

The criminal class simply reverted their operations back to gambling, extortion and loan-sharking. The next big payday era would become illegal drug distribution.

The Rome Coffee Shop, scene of the Volpe bloodbath would be closed permanently later due to unpaid rent. The building subsequently became a junk shop, numbers joint, fortune telling studio and finally a redevelopment casualty. The former gangster headquarters is currently embedded underneath a section of the PPG Paints Arena south parking lot.

Frank Manna's Barbershop is currently on the site of the BNY Mellon Client Service Center. The entire neighborhood is a massive construction project. Those buildings form the era still remaining will not be lingering much longer.

The legacy of the Volpe Brothers is primarily forgotten except among certain families within Wilmerding. The suburb was once a packed immigrant community of 6,400. The current population has splintered to approximately 2,000.

The formerly essential foundries and machine shops of the Westinghouse Air Brake Company are no longer functioning. They've become ruins zealously cloaked by phantoms.

The Crumbling of a Mayoral Fiefdom
Site of Former Pittsburgh City Hall: Corner of Smithfield
and Oliver Way *(Currently Mellon Square)*, **Pittsburgh**

Timing and turmoil decimated the tenure and health of Charles H. Kline, Pittsburgh's 47th Mayor. Kline may have been one of Pittsburgh's most professionally qualified mayors. His reign was exceptional because he became was the last Republican mayor ever elected.

He was born in 1870 in Indiana County and attended the University of Pennsylvania. He became a lawyer in 1898 before his election to the Pennsylvania House of Representatives in 1904. Following his House victory, he was elected to the State Senate three years later. He served three terms and was the *President pro tempore* during the 1915 session. He then became a judge in the state courts from 1919 to 1925.

He was elected Pittsburgh's mayor in 1926 and immediately encountered a major legal obstacle with Prohibition. The unpopular law never gained a local foothold. Police and civic authority corruption achieved dangerous heights. Kline's reputation swirled amidst the toxic vortex.

Pittsburgh was affected deeply by the Great Depression, but despite the commercial hardships, the corporate community expanded. Major skyscrapers including the Gulf Oil Tower, Grant Building and Koppers Tower elevated the downtown skyline. During his administration, Pittsburgh annexed the neighboring suburb of Carrick.

For seven turbulent years, the embattled Kline weathered personal attacks against his administration. The incidental purchase of an oriental rug crowned a 48-count series of indictments against him. He was convicted and ordered to resign on March 31, 1933. He faced a six-month long imprisonment that he would never serve.

His character was shredded and his morale dissipated. He died at St. Francis Hospital on July 22, 1933. Prohibition would officially conclude later that year on December 5th.

**Louis Volpe: The Final Remnant of a Local Crime Family
Prohibition Headquarters: Penn-Shady Hotel *(Currently
The Cavendish Hotel)*
226 Shady Avenue, Pittsburgh**

Louis Volpe was imprisoned inside the Allegheny County
Jailhouse when three of his brothers were mercilessly gunned
down blocks away on Friday, July 29, 1932. He was briefly
released from his cell and allowed to pay his family respects
before their burial procession.

He had become ensnared and incarcerated during December
1931 by a Prohibition agent sting operation. He'd sold a pair
of agents a 5-gallon jug of whiskey for $16 and another a pint
for 50 cents.

Upon his eventual release, Pittsburgh's gangster terrain had
altered radically. All former crime patriarchs had uniformly
been murdered including his briefly reining brothers.

His sole remaining memory was his brother John's luxurious
light green Cadillac fortified with bulletproof windows. He
continued to pilot the distinctive vehicle roaming the Hill
District. He evaded impounding efforts by the car dealership
still owed for the initial purchase. He attempted to rejuvenate
the family's bootlegging enterprise operating from the Shady-
Penn Hotel.

The reincarnation failed miserably.

He and his brother Joseph were arrested twice for assault
against owners refusing to lease their warehouses to them for
liquor storage. Both brothers remained in jail because they
were unable to afford bail.

The April 7, 1933 repeal of Prohibition prompted his
immediate shift to less lucrative and more conventional

enterprises. His brother Guy died from a paralytic stroke on April 8, 1934 attributed to alcohol consumption. His father Ignazzio would pass away on August 18, 1936 on a small farm near his birthplace in Agropoli, Italy. He had returned to his homeland in 1929 while his sons were ascending to local criminal prominence. Perhaps his motivation was shame for the legacy that he had sired.

The once volatile Louis mellowed with time and aging. During the 1960s, his more legitimate business supplied cigarettes for vending machines. He acquired an ownership interest in the White Oak Rainbow Garden Amusement Park.

During his declining years, he evolved into a de-clawed and toothless lion. He became a fixture sitting habitually on a Wilmerding park bench, waving and chatting amicably with friends and passing pedestrians. He died from kidney failure on June 5, 1987 at Shadyside Hospital.

A Passenger Train Spills From the Elevated Tracks
Train Accident Site:
Merchant and Martindale Streets, Pittsburgh

Running fast and 20 minutes late during inclement weather, a Pennsylvania Railroad train arriving from Akron, Ohio jumped the track on February 26, 1934 at 9:32 p.m. The train turned over at the intersection of Merchant and Martindale Streets on the North Side. The locomotive, tender and five coaches tumbled down the elevated culvert. The coaches spilled onto the street while destroying an electrical substation. An entire corner and wall were demolished at the adjacent D. L. Clark candy factory.

The train was only three minutes from arriving at the North Side's Fort Wayne station when it jumped a frozen switch. Many of the 57 passengers inside were booked on extension continuations to Philadelphia and New York City.

Darkness and cold made escape difficult and hampered rescue efforts. Injured passengers were rushed to nearby Allegheny and Presbyterian Hospitals. Another train coach would be positioned adjacent to the wreckage to assist as an on-site hospital.

The train engineer and fireman along with seven passengers were killed. The dead were either seated in the initial coach or last sleeper car. Swinging upper berths when their car overturned crushed them. Many became so entangled that they couldn't be freed until railroad crews could extricate their bodies using welding cutting torches hours later.

The Clark Candy Company remained closed due to widespread damage until repairs could be completed. Power generators were shattered, electric lines violently ripped out and tracks leading to the shipping department destroyed.

he D.L. CLARK Company

An Educational Tower Extending to the Heavens
University of Pittsburgh Cathedral of Learning
4200 Fifth Avenue, Pittsburgh

The University of Pittsburgh's Cathedral of Learning originally appeared as a looming spacecraft mysteriously planted in the midst of their main campus. The surrounding Oakland neighborhood has since added several high rises. The 42-story gothic skyscraper dominates everything nearby. It is the second-tallest gothic-styled structure in the world after Manhattan's Woolworth Building.

The construction process of *Cathy* nicknamed by Pitt students is an extended narrative. The building was commissioned in 1921, but ground wasn't broken until 1926. Due to financial delays imposed by the Great Depression, its exterior would not be fully completed until October 1934. Its formal dedication was delayed an additional three years.

The Cathedral of Learning is a steel framed structure with Indiana limestone coating the exterior. The interior features distinguished examples of stained glass, stone, wood and ironworks. It contains in excess of 2,000 rooms and windows. The building is employed primarily for classrooms and administrative offices. Numerous subject departments are headquartered inside.

A studio theatre, event hall, computer and language labs, food court, study lounges, and custom designed specialty spaces distinguish its varied employment. The top of the building serves as the transmitter for a student operated radio station.

The proposed height of the building created immediate controversy. Many local residents and some university officials felt the summit excessive. A prevailing legend suggested that then University chancellor John Bowman ordered the fitting of the limestone walls to begin at the top floor and work downwards. The rationale was this method of construction would insure that the project could not be shortened or canceled.

The stonework was actually started on the ground floor before being continued on the upper levels. The limestone was not intentioned to be load bearing, so the order and level of placement became irrelevant. The biggest challenge facing fitting was that the designated stone quarry could not adhere to delivery deadlines. Work was shifted to the higher levels earlier as a consequence.

During World War II, a bomb threat was revealed against the structure necessitating extra guards to prevent sabotage. Twelve floors of the building were dedicated towards military use from 1943 until 1945. The Cathedral housed, fed and instructed nearly 1,000 members of the Army Air Corps (later renamed the Air Force) and Army engineers.

Early Allegheny County Airport Woes
Allegheny County Airport
12 Allegheny County Airport, West Mifflin

Commercial air travel during the earliest era of flying was characterized by diminutive passenger loads, but fraught with danger. Allegheny County Airport suffered a litany of four fatal accidents between 1935-1937.

The series of calamities began on January 26, 1935 when a Consolidated Fleetster aircraft on an airmail run crashed in an adjacent slag mound shortly following take off. The cause was determined to be icing on the wings. The impact resulting in a fire that destroyed the plane and mail sacks along with killing the pilot unable to escape.

Ten months later on November 16, a Stinson Model A craft operated by Central Airlines crashed during takeoff due to engine failure. All three individuals on board survived, a rare occurrence then in plane mishaps.

On April 7, 1936, TWA Flight #1 was en route to Pittsburgh as part of its regularly scheduled Sun Racer circuit. The flight originated from Newark, New Jersey with its final destination intended for Los Angeles making a dozen intermediate stops. Pittsburgh was the second stop on the itinerary. The Douglas DC-2 crashed near Uniontown after the pilot lost contact with the airport's radio navigation signal.

The plane veered several miles off course in a southwestern line. Thick fog shrouded the region. The pilot fearing wing icing lowered the plane in an attempt to find visual landmarks to navigate with. The aircraft struck several ice-covered trees atop Cheat Mountain, 40 miles south of Pittsburgh straddling the West Virginia border.

The impact instantly killed the two pilots and ten of the passengers and crew aboard. Flight attendant Nellie Granger was able to save two passengers despite her own severe injuries. One of the passengers would die subsequently.

On September 5, 1936, a Stinson 6000 tri-motor craft operating under the name Skyways crashed near the Allegheny Airport while on a sightseeing flight. Nine of the ten passengers and crew aboard were killed. The lone survivor became the earliest known example of a sole survivor from a commercial aviation accident.

The final catastrophe occurred on March 25, 1937 with TWA Flight #15A when the aircraft crashed into a gully in Clifton, approximately 7 miles south of Pittsburgh. The flight was a regularly scheduled route from Newark, New Jersey to Pittsburgh via Camden, New Jersey.

Extra fuel had been loaded aboard prior to the Camden departure. The fuel would enable the plane to continue to Columbus, Ohio in the event weather conditions prevented a Pittsburgh landing. Some passengers were denied boarding due to the extra weight.

The flight proceeded uneventfully and the control tower had given landing instructions to the pilot. These instructions became their final communications.

Another TWA pilot taking off observed the impending disaster from his nearby ascending plane. Instead of initiating the left turn requested by the control tower, he observed that the plane began a series of leftward spirals before crashing into the ground nose first. The observing pilot steered his plane away to prevent his passengers from viewing the wreckage. He then notified airport officials. All thirteen passengers and crewmembers aboard Flight #15A would perish from the crash.

A Predictable Pittsburgh Winter Malady

It is difficult to measure the worst natural flooding catastrophe in Pittsburgh. Their historical frequency is common particularly throughout the downtown and former Fort Pitt (currently Point Park) region. The convergence of the Allegheny and Monongahela Rivers creates the ideal basin for rising water levels to overlap onto lower lands offering no alternative escape valve.

Since 1763, over thirty documented occurrences of sustained flooding have plagued central Pittsburgh. The 1936 St. Patrick's Day inundation is considered perhaps the worst. On March 16th, two inches of rain fell that were coupled by warm temperatures rapidly melting an accumulated winter snowpack of 63 inches.

On unlucky St. Patrick's Day, rising waters breached installed barricades and streamed into the downtown streets. The surge reached a peak level of 46 feet at the Point, radically exceeding the recognized flood stage of 20 feet. That level still remains the highest historically recorded level.

Lacking an immediate exit valve, the waters required a week to recede. The damage and devastation was enormous throughout the entire Western Pennsylvania region. Over 62 people were reported dead, 500 injured and 135,000 remained homeless. Millions of dollars in reparations were required. The timing coincided with other severe financial ravages imposed by the Great Depression. Certain downtown buildings still have water stains from the flood.

The measure of havoc and devastation may have never been quite equaled, but late winter flooding remains an acknowledged hazard and reality.

HELLO

**The Outing of a Klansman and His Continuing Legacy
Appraisal
Pittsburgh Post-Gazette Headquarters:
34 Boulevard of the Allies, Pittsburgh**

Hugo Black was a Birmingham, Alabama based lawyer during the first quarter of the twentieth century. He specialized in labor law and personal injury cases. In 1927, he would be elected to the U.S. Senate representing his state for the next ten years.

Upon the retirement of conservative Supreme Court Justice Willis Van Devanter in 1937, President Franklin Roosevelt sought to appoint an alternative type of replacement. He searched for a younger aged justice supportive of his New Deal policies and originating from a region of the country not represented by the court.

He narrowed his search to three men and ultimately nominated Hugo Black. The other two candidates, Stanley Reed and Sherman Minton would eventually become Supreme Court justices. Roosevelt admired Black's Senate voting record, his early support of him and proactive energy towards reform.

On August 12, 1937 Roosevelt officially nominated Black, but instead of rubber-stamping his choice (as was the normal policy then), the Senate referred his nomination to the Judiciary Committee. Lingering rumors of Black's past affiliation with bigotry-oriented groups tainted his reputation.

Black's defense against the charge was citing an earlier law case where he'd intervened on behalf of a black defendant. The defendant had experienced previous due process violations. This modest character reference example would evolve into a vetting nightmare for Roosevelt. The President indicated that he was unaware of any past history that might derail the nomination.

The Judiciary Committee voted to recommend Black's candidacy. The Senate then voted in favor 63-16 to approve his nomination. Opposition came from ten Republicans and six Democrats. Alabama Governor Bibb Graves would appoint his own wife to complete Black's vacated Senate seat.

On September 13, 1937, *Pittsburgh Post-Gazette* writer Ray Springle initiated a series of articles documenting Black's 1920s membership and involvement with the Ku Klux Klan. The articles prompted Black into a fumbling admission of his prior Klan association. He claimed that *before becoming a Senator, I dropped the Klan*, dating his action to 1925.

National response was immediate, vehement and furious towards Black. Springle's articles prompted numerous demands for Black's immediate resignation. Springle would be honored with a Pulitzer Prize for his exposé in 1938. Black survived the storm. He would remain the first of Roosevelt's nine justices appointed during his presidency.

Hugo Black became the fifth longest serving justice in Supreme Court history. Observers consider him one of the most liberal and influential members during the 20th century. His reform philosophy reinforced many of Roosevelt's controversial New Deal policies.

Two major decisions during his tenure tested his racial impartiality. Black was one of nine Supreme Court justices that in 1954 voted against segregation in public schools. In 1965, he joined a unanimous court decision in overruling the dismissal of murder and conspiracy charges by a trial court against eighteen Ku Klux Klan members. The men would be retried with seven found guilty.

Hugo Black would remain in his justice position towards the end of his life at the age of 85. In August 1971, he admitted himself into the National Naval Medical Center and officially resigned his office on September 17th. Two days later he suffered a stroke and would die on September 25th.

Posthumously, he was honored on a U.S. postage stamp. In 1987, the Birmingham U.S. District courthouse building was named after him.

Controversy has not eluded his legacy even following his death. His prior association with the Ku Klux Klan will *never* become forgotten. Protestors and organizations periodically express their ire over his courthouse naming by defacement and picketing.

Time will continue to shape an overall perception of his legacy. One bold Pittsburgh reporter enabled Americans to know a confirmed truth regarding his early background. Whether Black's subsequent legal decisions will merit forgiveness may require generations to determine.

**Island Queen Steamer Explosion
Monongahela Wharf Landing
200-298 Fort Pitt Boulevard, Pittsburgh**

The *Island Queen* steamship was christened on April 19, 1925 at Cincinnati's Public Landing. Originally intended to be powered by coal, it was later converted to burn oil. The 1,000 horsepower steam engines were supplied in Cincinnati with the boiler and smokestacks manufactured in Gallipolis, Ohio.

The side-wheel steel-hull excursion boat carried passengers to and from Coney Island in Cincinnati during the peak summer season. Afterwards, the routing became Pittsburgh until New Orleans. The steamer measured 285 feet long by 45 feet wide. The side wheels were 30 feet in diameter and the ship's fully loaded capacity was 4,000 people. The boat weighed 1,000 tons and contained six boilers.

On Labor Day, September 1, 1947, the *Island Queen* would depart Coney Island for its scheduled routing to Pittsburgh.

On September 9th, the boat was docked along the Monongahela Wharf for repairs. At 1:16 p.m., the ship's chief engineer intended to weld a loose deck-stanchion, a metal brace running from deck to ceiling. He lit a welding torch near an oil storage tank. Unaware of vapors emitting from the oil tank, the ignited torch immediately flashed flames throughout the structure.

Two explosions ripped across the bow of the steamer. The first ruptured a fuel line prompting the second. The fire spread immediately and lethally, as 27,000 gallons of fuel were stored onboard. Approximately 86 of the 90-person crew were believed to be aboard making preparations for that evening's moonlight excursion. No passengers were aboard at the time. The night before, the ship had accommodated a fully booked 4,000-passenger load.

Several of the crew leapt into the Monongahela River or were blown into the waters by the force of the explosion. Twenty-four crewmembers were trapped below. Nineteen would ultimately die including the chief engineer. Eighteen others would be reported injured with thirteen requiring hospitalization. Approximately 40-parked automobiles were damaged along the waterfront. Office windows were blown out from the adjacent business district.

Amidst the chaos and destruction, divers scanned the murky waters in a vain attempt to locate all of the victim's bodies.

The 1947 version of the *Island Queen* was a second incarnation. The original burned to the waterline while in dry-dock during 1922. That destruction left no casualties.

Several hours after the second *Island Queen* exploded, the remains would settled into approximately 12 feet of water at the bottom. A salvage operation would ultimately follow.

On April 10, 1948, the ship was officially announced as being scrapped due to the permanent and irreparable damage to the hull. On the other side of the Monongahela River, steamship and paddlewheel boats still sail the river seasonally.

A Second Chance At Life Squandered During The Same Day
Emsworth Locks and Dams, Ohio River

On April 19, 1948, Howard Miller, 31, cheated death once, but would not a second time. Earlier in the day, his motorboat stalled near the Emsworth Locks and Dams. Flight instructor Roberta Wastel landed her pontoon-equipped plane near Miller's drifting craft. He had been powerless to prevent the boat from being swept over the 10-foot high dam.

Safely steered to shore, Miller decided to return to navigating the Ohio River two hours later. As he was accelerating the craft's speed, the boat overturned. Miller's body would never be recovered and he was presumed to have drowned.

Two Bizarre Accidents Plague A Country Club
Montour Heights Country Club
1491 Coraopolis Height Road, Coraopolis

The Montour Heights Country Club is located on property that was part of the McCune family estate. The club's origins trace back to 1911 when first founded by a group of local residents. The construction of a 9-hole golf course was completed the following year. In 1987, additional acreage was acquired to expand the facility.

Two odd accidents have plagued the property beginning with a July 14, 1950 chartered plane crash on the fairway following an awkward emergency landing. Two passengers, one the treasurer of the Copperfield Steel Company and his friend were incinerated following the impact. The pilot was burned on the hands and arms as he attempted to rescue the pair.

An even odder calamity occurred on Friday morning, September 8, 2017. The body of a man along with his vehicle was discovered inside the murky waters of the golf course pond. The course groundskeeper first sighted the head and shoulders of the man sticking up out of the water. While divers were retrieving his cadaver, the car was also located in the depths.

The victim would be identified as local resident Roy Sanders, 50, who'd last been seen by family members four days before. As investigators pieced together a strange sequence of events, it was believed that Sander's vehicle had struck a utility pole on Tuesday morning. Police had found car parts littered from the collision along the road, but no sign of the vehicle.

Investigators speculated that the vehicle continued on a path through a First Baptist church parking lot, and then followed sloping terrain before sliding into the pond approximately 400 yards away. In all probability, Sanders had been dead three days underneath the water.

The crash coincided only hours before his girlfriend was giving birth to their son Joseph, their third child together. She speculated due to a heart condition that he may have suffered a fatal heart attack leading up to the collision.

A Defiant Victim of A Blind Anti-Communist Movement
Taylor Alderdice High School:
2409 Shady Avenue, Pittsburgh

On February 9, 1950, Wisconsin Senator Joseph McCarthy gave a Lincoln Day speech to the Republican Women's Club of Wheeling, West Virginia. The talk was credited with launching his infamous anti-Communist campaign that evolved into a nationwide *red scare*.

McCarthy's speech boasted that he possessed a list of known Communists Party Members working for the State Department. No such list existed. During the next four years, he would continue his exaggerations and attempt to discredit all potential adversaries and critics. It was a dark period of American politics. McCarthy insinuated that a deadly enemy existed *within* America, but he was dreadfully short on proof.

His censure by the Senate on December 2, 1954 effectively ended his reign of terror. The carnage resulted in suicides and many individuals, careers and reputations becoming tarnished beyond repair.

Dorothy Albert was a tenured eighteen-year English teacher at Pittsburgh's Taylor Alderdice High School. She became one of the initial casualties resulting from McCarthy's 1950 speech in Wheeling. Albert was a member of the Civil Right Congress, an association labeled to be aligned with extreme left-wing leanings.

Albert would be fired from her teaching position on February 7, 1951 for *Communist sympathies*. She contended that her dismissal was a violation of her constitutional right to free speech, expression and association. That same year, the Pennsylvania state legislature would pass the Pennsylvania Loyalty Act on December 22nd affecting all public employees within the state.

She would appeal her case through the Allegheny County Commons Court. In November 1952, the U.S. Supreme Court would dismiss her appeal.

Albert's defiant refusal to accept the school's decision was a personal stance based on principle. At the time of her dismissal, she became a victim of an emerging mass movement lacking in-depth research towards who might legitimately constitute a threat.

Dorothy Albert was no menace to American freedom. She was an educator disgraced, discarded and ultimately forgotten locally.

**A Routine Car Collision and Freak Gas Explosion
Decimates A Family
Former Accident Site: Bottom of Troy Hill Road Steps
(Formerly 1402 East Ohio Street), Pittsburgh**

At approximately 11:00 p.m. on December 5, 1952, John Liput, 17, was driving to his home in Arnold from Ohio State University. His car skidded on East Ohio Street due to the icy road conditions and he smashed into a concrete retaining wall in front of Robert Moulis' three-story residence. Liput was uninjured from the impact.

Thirteen minutes later, Moulis telephoned the Equitable Gas Company to request an inspection of a visibly damaged gas line for possible leakage. The gas company indicated that they would send out a crew to investigate. The impact from the collision had bent an exposed gas line running directly into the Moulis' home.

Prior to the collision, Robert Moulis and his wife Rose were occupied with putting their six children to bed. Four were already tucked in upstairs and two were watching a boxing match on the downstairs living room television. One of them, their only daughter Louise, 11, tired of viewing the fight. She began walking up the staircase towards her room. She shouted to her parents that she had just seen a car accident outside their house.

No one felt any unusual alarm.

At 11:30 p.m., the house abruptly exploded into a fireball. By the time that the gas company crew had arrived the house was engulfed in flames. Robert Moulis and his wife were dragged through the ruins to safety along with a tenant. Within three minutes, entry into the structure became impossible even for the fire crew. All six of the couple's children would be incinerated resulting in every parent's worst nightmare.

Following the events, Pittsburgh's Building Department and the Equitable Gas Company would distance themselves from the tragedy. The Superintendent of Building Inspection flatly stated in print: *The city does not supervise installation of gas lines*.

A coroner's jury returned a verdict of *accidental death*. The six children, ages 4-13 were mourned at a funeral service located at the Saint Nicholas Croatian Church on their same Ohio Street block.

Although cleared of criminal charges by the jury, the gas company was not fully discharged from responsibility. The Moulis couple sued the Equitable Gas Company for negligence in their gas line installation. In 1955, a jury awarded them $322,000. They eventually settled the case for $127,500.

The money enabled Robert Moulis to quit his job as a purchasing agent for a truck line. He invested in a fast food business partnership opening McDonald's restaurants throughout the region. The venture expanded into 30 restaurants before he retired and liquidated his share in 1988.

The location of the former Moulis residence is currently at the base of the Troy Hill Road Steps. The steps are closed to public access. East Ohio Street has been widened into four-lane Highway 28 and is more commonly known as the Pittsburgh-Buffalo Highway. Saint Nicholas Church was razed in January 2013. The windows and artifacts were removed three months before.

Two years following the tragedy, the Moulis would have another daughter, Rosemarie. The couple steadily launched themselves into charitable fundraising. They would secure thousands of dollars for Pittsburgh's Children's Hospital including funding a facility library.

Rose would die from lung cancer in 1997 with Robert surviving her until May 2008. He died at 92 from heart and kidney failure in Sudbury, Massachusetts.

The couple's unbearable grief made their role as benefactors even more exemplary. They'd survived an unimaginable horror and still were able to give generously to others within their lifetime.

A Test Vaccination Program With Global Implications Arsenal Elementary School:

215 39th Street, Pittsburgh

There are numerous parallels between the polio epidemic of the first half of the twentieth century and the recent COVID-19 pandemic. Polio did not accumulate an equal numbers of fatalities as Covid, but it was a highly contagious disease that spread in horrendous outbreaks. It was stubbornly resistant to various experimental treatments during that era. Polio attacked the nerve cells and often the central nervous system. It caused muscle deterioration, paralysis and death.

The most visible casualty was wheelchair bound President Franklin Roosevelt who'd survived the disease in 1921. Then, he was a rising politician. The disease attacked and spread quickly leaving his legs permanently paralyzed.

There are two primary differences between polio and Covid. Polio affects primarily children. During the mid-century, the concept of politicizing disease seemed unthinkable. The objective within medical research circles then was to discover a cure, not appease a President or political party.

Dr. Jonas Salk accepted a professorship at the School of Medicine from the University of Pittsburgh in 1947. He undertook a project to identify the number of variations of poliovirus. His research uncovered 125 strains of three basic types. For the subsequent seven years, he focused on developing a vaccine against the virus. The key component of his vaccine was a chemical called formalin that effectively deactivated the virus.

On February 23, 1954, a group of students from Arsenal Elementary School received the first injections of his polio vaccine. The testing was still in the experimental stage and the stakes were elevated. Failure with his vaccine meant additional years of research and trial and error.

Fortunately, Salk's vaccine worked. The vaccine would be released to the pubic in April 1955. In the present day, polio cases have been eradicated by 99% globally. Over time, perhaps the COVID inoculations will have a similar success rate.

One of the most impressive distinctions regarding Jonas Salk was that he chose not to patent the vaccine or seek any profit form his research in order to speed and maximize worldwide distribution. Such selflessness would be inconceivable today. Polio has become a standard immunization for children without controversy. Sadly the COVID vaccination has not.

Salk attempted to distance himself from the accompanying renown and celebrity of his accomplishment. The task proved Herculean. He would be feted and receive honors worldwide. In 1963, he founded the Salk Institute for Biological Studies in La Jolla, California. The organization continues today as a major center for medical and scientific research. Salk expanded his own research and published findings until shortly before his death at 80 in June 1995.

**A Christmas Flight Ditched Into The Monongahela
Clairton-Glassport Bridge, Glassport**

On December 22, 1954, a chartered Douglas C47A airplane
was flying 23 military personnel and crew to Tacoma,
Washington for the Christmas holidays. The flight had
originally departed from Newark, New Jersey with three
intermediate stops scheduled including Pittsburgh.

As the aircraft headed towards Pittsburgh, pilot Harold Poe
sensed that he might lack sufficient fuel to reach the
Allegheny County Airport. Communications between the
airport control tower and Poe proved troublesome. The
control tower suggested refueling at the Johnson,
Pennsylvania Airport, but Poe decided to attempt to land at
his preferred destination. His decision fatally crowned a
doomed series of miscalculations.

He almost arrived, but his dwindling fuel supply betrayed
him.   Nearing 11:00 p.m., his ten-year old aircraft was
approaching only three miles away from the airport. An air
traffic controller provided him landing instructions for
runway 27. The temperature outside was a frigid 20 degrees,
but the wind conditions were stable.

Poe conclusively decided that he lack sufficient fuel to reach
the runway and aborted his original intention. At 2,000 feet,
he made a left turn toward the south disappearing from the air
controller's view.

At the approximate location of the current Clairton-Glassport
Bridge, he landed the aircraft wheels up in the middle of the
Monongahela River. Rescue efforts saved over half of the
personnel on board. Nine passengers plus Harold Poe would
drown.

Investigators would later blame the fuel exhaustion problem on inadequate flight planning and insufficient crew supervision and training. The same report indicated that the flight had been overloaded at the time of takeoff. For numerous military families, the 1954 Christmas holiday became memorable for all the wrong reasons.

A Ghost Bomber Plunges Mysteriously Into the Monongahela River
Homestead Grays Bridge, Pittsburgh

At the height of the American Cold War with the Soviet Union, an American bomber plunged into the icy Monongahela River. The accident spared most of its crew but the plane was never *officially* recovered.

It was the late afternoon of January 31, 1956 and pilot Major William Dotson was running dangerous low on fuel. He had initially requested permission to land at the Pittsburgh International Airport, but became uncertain that the plane lacked the fuel capacity to arrive safely. He modified his request to the Allegheny County Airport.

Unfortunately, his B-25 Mitchell bomber became fully emptied of fuel and his engine began malfunctioning. He decided to splash land the craft wheels up on the surface of the Monongahela.

His airplane glided silently landing just past the Homestead Grays Bridge. All six crewmembers survived the impact and began floating with the plane for 11 minutes in the frigid 34-degree waters. Four of the men would be rescued, but two drowned as they attempted to swim to shore. Their bodies would require months to recover.

The U.S. Coast Guard cutter, the *Forsythia*, precariously attached a wing of the submerged plane while dragging its anchor. The line slipped and the entire plane slid to the estimated twenty-foot bottom.

What would have appeared to be an elementary retrieval never was published as being completed. The bomber eluded recovery despite the water's shallow depth. The U.S. Coast Guard and Army Corps of Engineers conducted search efforts for the 15-foot high plane for two weeks.

Their inability and the exact nature of the aircraft soon became shrouded in speculation and mystery. The purported routine training flight had departed Nellis Air Force Base in Nevada to retrieve a cargo of airplane parts at Olmstead Air Force Base in Harrisburg. The plane had refueled once at Tinker Air Force Base in Oklahoma.

Many observers speculated the plane might have been carrying dangerous cargo or even possibly a nuclear weapon. The fear of such revelation may have prompted the military into an immediate and clandestine retrieval operation the evening of the crash.

The Ghost bomber's landing location has never been publicly pinpointed despite extensive search efforts, sonar scanning and even eyewitness reports. One reported theory was that the airplane may have drifted with the currents and settled into a submerged gravel pit area in significantly deeper water. That site may have conceivably covered the craft in over 10-15 feet of silt.

**An Extended Pittsburgh Curse With Aviation Travel
Pittsburgh International Airport
1000 Airport Blvd., Pittsburgh**

Pittsburgh International Airport had only been opened four years when disaster struck on Easter Sunday, 1956. TWA Flight #400 was taking off at 7:00 p.m. heading towards Newark, New Jersey.

The Martin 404 aircraft began to lift off normally and then abruptly banked to the left and collided into a hillside adjacent to the airport. The plane impacted on its nose and the interior fittings broke loose. As the aircraft hit the ground, the wing fuel tanks ruptured and the plane erupted into flames.

The nearby crash site was visible to potential rescuers enabling many to run directly to the wreckage. The inferno became so intense, however, there was no way for them to assist. Firefighting crews were dispatched immediately but the torturous country roads leading to the crash site required twenty minutes to navigate.

Miraculously, fourteen people escaped the fractured fuselage to safety. Jumbled seats tossed within the cracked interior impeded their efforts. Twenty-one passengers and a flight attendant would perish as the plane was completely consumed by the fire.

Investigators determined that a fire warning triggered by a loose exhaust clamp prompted the crash. The crew experienced a severe loss of power upon take off and then attempted an unsuccessful correction. The plane never elevated higher than 100 feet off the ground. The pilot had only ten seconds to react to the impending disaster.

Aviation within Pittsburgh historically has been tethered to a curse. Only three months earlier, a military B-25 Mitchell bomber had crash-landed into the Monongahela River killing two. The plane was never *officially* recovered. Less than two years earlier, a chartered military aircraft plunged into the inhospitable Monongahela waters further south near McKeesport. The Allegheny County Airport was afflicted by four fatal flights between the years 1935-1937.

The most memorable nearby disaster would not be associated with Pittsburgh. The catastrophe would take place on September 11, 2001. United Airlines Flight #93 would crash in rural Pennsylvania, approximately 80 miles east of Pittsburgh. The intended target for the airplane was speculated to be Washington D.C. and the U.S. Capitol building. Passengers on board overwhelmed the highjacking terrorists forcing the disaster on one of the nation's darkest days.

**A Whiz Kid Conning Investors With Traditional Tactics
First National Bank of Saltsburg:
214 Point Street, Saltsburg**

Earl Fleeger Belle might have become one of America's most revered business minds due to his apparent self-confidence and instinctive leadership. Instead, he became infamous as one of the most publicized stock and fraud manipulators during the 1950s.

He graduated from the University of Pittsburgh in 1956 and established the Eastern Investment Development Corporation with his father and two brothers. The group cultivated a redevelopment plan for the borough of Saltsburg. He became a director of the First National Bank locally.

His company's accelerated growth strategy began with purchasing control of American Stock Exchange listed company Cornucopia Mines in 1957. The company based in Washington State was financial defunct, but still listed. Belle inflated the value of this stock to acquire other companies. He named his new holding company General Kinetics.

Part of Belle's allure was his blatant swagger. He flew Pittsburgh newsmen, civic and business leaders to New York City. He entertained them with a string orchestra and the finest whiskey served by the city's loveliest *hostesses*, an euphemism for prostitutes.

He drove a Jaguar, a Mercedes and a White Cadillac. He rented helicopters to escort Long Island bankers and potential investors to Saltsburg to view a charade he'd orchestrated. He had rented a battalion of construction equipment for a day to appear working on a nonexistent company owned building site.

The babyish appearing Belle was reciprocated with praise,

credibility and showered with superlatives for his *genius*. He'd fooled nearly everyone except bank examiners. His façade would rapidly collapse in the summer of 1958.

One of his company's acquisitions included the Manufacturers Bank of Edgewater, New Jersey in April 1958. The bank collapsed three months later after it was determined that an excess of $150,000 had been siphoned off to Belle.

Earl Belle didn't linger for an indictment against him. He left his family and partners to shoulder the responsibility. He fled Pittsburgh symbolically on July 4th with $1 million. He was eventually sighted in Rio de Janeiro, Brazil. He was charged in absentia on 17 counts of conspiracy, mail fraud and violation of federal banking laws. His father, brothers and assorted partners would all face criminal charges and receive modest prison sentences and fines.

One million dollars in 1958 would have appeared an enormous financial cushion. He remarried for a third time and surrounded himself with a legion of household servants. By the early 1960s, his money had evaporated. Belle was charged with passing worthless checks in Brazil.

He voluntarily returned to the United States in December 1963 one month before an extradition treaty would have forced him back.

Belle pleaded guilty to 26 counts of falsifying financial records and fraud. He pleaded no defense to 18 additional counts. He served 22 months of a 30-month sentence before his release in May 1966.

The *Pittsburgh Whiz Kid* was now a 34-year old forgotten novelty. Following his release, he began employment with his father as a shoe salesman. The mundane and conventional could never suit him. He reportedly returned to scamming before being obliged to disappear once again.

Earl Belle always sought the expedient path to wealth regardless of consequence or whom he injured. There was always a promising future he sensed even amidst the bleakest reality.

In 1981, the Security Exchange Commission (SEC) sanctioned him in connection with his questionable dealings with Teletrans Industries. Numerous German investors within the company sued him. He was incapable of remorse or guilt and eventually died despised in Florida on April 3, 1995.

A Ten-Year-Old Shoots His Abusive Father to Death
Chervenak Residence:
8438 Dersam Street, Pittsburgh

Michael *Mickey* Chervenak had witnessed and experienced sufficient violence from his abusive father. On September 6, 1957, the 10-year-old had spent the day fishing with his father who shared the same name. His 31-year-old father was employed at U.S. Steel's Edgar Thomson plant in Braddock.

That evening his father began drinking from a six-pack of beer that he'd purchased earlier that day. He had nearly finished half when he became irate. His wife served him eggs accompanied by corn for dinner. He threw the meal at her and began shouting about the extent of his hatred towards her.

He then became physically violent. He slapped her multiple times and continued choking her until finally she was able to wrest herself free. It was common occurrence in the Chervenak household. Mickey tried to intervene, but was overpowered, spanked with a belt and slapped across the face.

His father's abuse had blackened the family's regard towards him with paralyzing fear. Mickey decided that the beatings had to cease, particularly towards his mother and younger sister.

Two weeks earlier his father had purchased a 12-gauge shotgun because an intruder had tried to break into their home. He taught Mickey how to use it. The weapon was concealed under his parent's bed.

Mickey ran upstairs, loaded the rifle and rested it on the banister awaiting his father's approach into the living room. The rifle length was nearly his height. His father entered the doorway and Mickey blasted him from only a foot away. The bullet created a 2 1/2 inch crater in his father's chest killing him instantly.

Mickey's age and the reported abusive background behind the shooting made riveting headlines across the United States. Everyone with the exception of the decease's two sisters and their family found his story heartbreaking.

The sisters defended their brother insisting that Mickey had lied. They accused Mickey's mother of the shooting and his story merely covered up for her actions. They maintained that their brother's wife had never given him a *proper* home.

The evidence and investigating detectives collaborated with Mickey's account of events. A jury agreed unanimously to rule the case a *justifiable homicide*. Mickey was released to his mother's care. A homemaker, she was left nearly financially destitute.

Her husband's will consisted of a single asset, the family's 1956 Chevy sedan valued at $700. She would file a request with the Allegheny County Coroner's office to return the rifle that Mickey had used to shoot his father. It was delivered the following day.

The Chervenak family never reconciled with her or the two children. Their ill feelings were shared mutually.

In her final Pittsburgh media interview following the trial, she expressed concern regarding her family's future.

Her fears proved justified. Mickey struggled with extreme bouts of depression and guilt throughout the remainder of his life. The scars of abusive left by his father remained etched irretrievably inside his soul. He would die in Florida during 2018.

**A Children's Legendary Television Pioneer
Television Station WQED:
4802 Fifth Avenue, Pittsburgh**

The fantasy universe of Fred Rogers' resulted in a 1962 Canadian CBC Television series called *Misterrogers*. Four years later, the show re-titled *Mister Rogers' Neighborhood* was produced by Pittsburgh broadcaster WQED and shown nationally via public broadcasting stations. The half-hour educational series was oriented towards children 2 to 5, but attracted a wider aged audience.

Rogers' began his television career in 1953 at WQED with partner host Josie Carey hosting *The Children's Corner*. The program featured Rogers as puppeteer and composer with Carey as host and lyricist. The unscripted live program screened during weekday afternoons. The show captured a Sylvania Award, that era's equivalent of an Emmy and was briefly broadcast on the NBC Television Network.

The Children's Corner would introduce many of the puppets, characters and music employed with his later production. The show also introduced him wearing tennis shoes that were motivated by practicality. Tennis shoes proved much quieter on the set than more formal varieties, as he was moving around constantly behind the set.

The *Mister Rogers* series maintained a consistent format with Rogers often speaking directly to his viewers on various topics. He periodically strayed into controversial material including divorce, anger, fear, competition, death and war. Fred Rogers attempted to make a clear distinction between the realistic world of his Oakland television neighborhood and his fabricated world of make-believe.

In 1967, the series would be cancelled due to a lack of funding, but extensive public response prompted a fresh source. The Sears Roebuck Foundation became the program's financial savior enabling national broadcast distribution on the National Education Television (NET) and later replacement distributor Public Broadcast Station (PBS).

In May 1997, the series surpassed *Captain Kangaroo* as the longest-running children's television series. In June 2003, Sesame Street would ellipse Mister Rogers' record. The final episode was taped on December 1, 2000, the fifth episode of the 31st season. The studio where the show was taped at WQED would be later renamed the *Fred Rogers Studio*.

Fred Rogers would die at his Pittsburgh home at the age of 74 on February 27, 2003. His cause of death was stomach cancer. The series would broadcast as reruns on most PBS stations until August 31, 2007. PBS permanently removed it from the daily syndicated schedule after August 29, 2008. His wife Joanne would die on January 14, 2021 at the age of 92.

The Elusive Commuter Bandit
William Zeiler's Grocery Store and Upstairs Apartment:
1336 Juniata Street, Pittsburgh

Over a period of four years, William Edward Zeiler committed reportedly 11 Pittsburgh bank robberies beginning in April 1963. He employed a consistent routine that varied little and seemingly should have made him easy to track.

He operated consistently on weekdays between noon and 3:30 p.m. earning the moniker of the *Commuter Bandit*. Zeiler would stroll into his targeted bank and request change, often a roll of quarters. He then would push a note and paper bag towards the teller demanding that all $5, $10 and $20 bills inside his/her drawer be placed inside the sack. He would display an automatic .45 caliber pistol to reinforce his earnestness and their discretion.

Over four years, police were provided with the identical description of the perpetrator. He was burly built at approximately 6 feet and 200-240 pounds. He had an oval, clean-shaven face, blues eyes and a sandy, receding hairline. He generally wore slacks, a sport shirt open at the neck, a jacket and cap.

He habitually drove an older model car that was usually stolen for his getaway. He would steer the vehicle afterwards to where his own car was parked and switch vehicles. During one of his most brazen getaways in July 1964, his stolen car engine caught fire. He calmly stopped in the middle of heavy traffic, exited and blended into the sidewalk pedestrian traffic. Several police cars including one containing FBI agents were only yards away in pursuit.

One of the prevailing theories regarding the *Commuter Bandit* was that he resided in the suburbs. The FBI and police would finally arrest him on June 23, 1967 in the Manchester district grocery store that he owned and operated. He and his family lived in an upstairs apartment. Zeiler would be identified in police line-ups by more than fifty of his victims.

He would be convicted and imprisoned in 1968, but granted a new trial by the U.S. Third Circuit Court of Appeals. The court ruled that witnesses who testified against him during his original trial were *legally incompetent*. In 1972, a federal court jury would convict Zeiler on three counts of bank robbery. He would be sentenced to eight and a half years imprisonment for each count.

He continued his appeals as his appearance steadily disappeared from headline news.

**Union Bridge: Excessively Low Clearance Prompts A Supreme Court Ruling
Fort Duquesne Bridge (Former Site of Union Bridge)**

The Union Bridge Company was conceived and incorporated in 1873 with the intention of constructing a span linking Pittsburgh with Allegheny. The crossing became the initial bridge to be constructed at Pittsburgh's Point on the Allegheny River side.

The completed bridge was built primarily of wood with a covered roof. Designers preferred wood due to their reservations regarding the quality and durability of iron. The Union Bridge would become the fourth and final completed covered span in Pittsburgh. None currently remain.

The bridge was opened to traffic on October 1, 1874. During this period a companion span called the Point Bridge was being planned across the Monongahela River side to Carson Street.

The construction was stationed upon four stone piers with elaborate portals on each extremity. The assemblage was connected in five equal spans and featured a two-lane roadway with double-tracks for trolley traffic and twin sidewalks. The toll for pedestrian crossings was one cent for men and complimentary for women and children under 14. Fees for horse drawn vehicles ranged between five and fifteen cents.

Despite presumed advance scrutiny, the opening revealed a significant design flaw. The clearance level of only thirty feet created enormous hardship for water navigation. The Union Bridge Company resisted modifications. Their obstinacy towards change ultimately resulted in future bridge constructions mandating a minimum clearance level of seventy feet.

The undersized level remained a hazard to river commerce and particularly the Point during flooding seasons. Litigation proved the sole solution.

The local Rivermen and the Pittsburgh Coal Exchange registered a lawsuit in 1902 and again two years later against the Union Bridge Company. The second suit ultimately reached the U.S. Supreme Court where the justices ruled in favor of the plaintiffs. The Supreme Court decision regarding clearance levels ultimately affected Pittsburgh's other bridges. By 1918, all of the major bridges were in compliance.

Despite the legal setback, the bridge remained intact until 1907. An extensive flood that year on March 15 when water levels rose to thirty-nine feet necessitated the bridge's closure and dismantling.

In the interim between the closure and the newly constructed North Side Point Bridge, ferries were used for pedestrians. Vehicles were diverted over to the Sixth Street Bridge.

The steel framed constructed Manchester Bridge replacement opened in August 1915. In 1970, that span would be demolished and replaced by the present day operating Fort Duquesne Bridge.

A Probable Suicide Prompted By A Cornered District Attorney
Allegheny County District Attorney Office:
436 Grant Street, Pittsburgh
Suicide Location:
Lochnoc Farms, Ligonier

Allegheny County District Attorney Robert W. Duggan was first elected to his position in January 1964. His father was the president of Consolidated Ice Company and the family lived in affluence. He was raised and educated in Pittsburgh and enlisted in the Air Force after high school towards the close of World War II.

Duggan would earn his undergraduate and law degree from the University of Pittsburgh. His predecessor as District Attorney was Edward *Easy Going* Boyle. Duggan eluded close scrutiny for his performance during his first two terms. He cultivated a perceived hard-line philosophy against crime and corruption.

His third term re-election and marriage to longtime companion Cordelia Scaife May in August 1973 changed that. May was an heiress to industrialist Andrew Mellon's family fortune.

During Duggan's ten-year tenure, the 48-year-old's progressive reputation featured one glaring omission. The county had minimal prosecutions for gambling related offenses. Pittsburgh has been historically known as a gambling vortex. The Internal Revenue Service and an ambitious United States Attorney for Western Pennsylvania Richard Thomburgh turned their investigative attention towards Duggan. In particular, they scoured his undocumented sources of income and relationship with regional criminal families.

On the morning of March 5, 1974, a Federal grand jury was scheduled to convene and indict Duggan for income tax fraud and evasion. The charges accused him of failing to report more than $137,000 in income during 1967-70. These sources reportedly originated as a series of protection payments collected from racketeers by Samuel Ferraro, Duggan's former chief detective. Ferraro had been convicted the previous year of failing to report bribes amounting to $390,000.

Duggan would never read the text of the indictment.

Hours before the charges were announced publicly, Duggan went hunting on his Ligonier family estate Lochnoc Farms. The property is secluded in the foothills of the Laurel Mountains.

Later that day, his body would be found on the grounds of the estate. A spent shotgun was located seven to ten feet from his body. There were immediate questions raised as to whether the shooting was accidental, murder or self-inflicted. The majority of observers felt that Duggan had turned the gun on himself. The landing distance of the weapon away from him raised serious, but ultimately unanswerable questions.

His wife, Cordelia Scaife May initially doubted the suicide theory and the corruption charges against her husband. She reportedly ultimately came to terms with accepting his duplicity and suicide. One of the wealthiest women in America, she died in her Ligonier home of pancreatic cancer at the age of 76 in 2005.

A Regional Stock Exchange Limited By A Growth Ceiling
Former Pittsburgh Stock Exchange Building:
333 Fourth Avenue, Pittsburgh

The Pittsburgh Oil Exchange was organized in 1864 based on oil traded as a commodity during the Civil War. The organization was also known regionally as Thurston's Oil Exchange. Six years later, it was alternatively called the Pittsburgh Coal Exchange. Standard Oil began a consolidation process of absorbing smaller exchanges during the 1870s. In 1878, the Pittsburgh exchange listed 180 actively trading members.

General stocks were included into the trading operations during 1894. Over the next two years, the formerly exclusive energy-trading platform was transformed into the Pittsburgh Stock Exchange.

The regional exchange was located within the Dollar Bank Building at 340 Fourth Avenue. That structure was destroyed by fire on October 29, 1896. A permanent headquarters would be established in 1903 in the former Mechanic's National Bank Building.

The exchange never cultivated sufficient growth or sustained traction during its history. Its volatile marketplace closed on several occasions during steep economic crises. During 1907, it ceased operations for three months during a recessionary period. On July 31, 1914, it would shutter for four months due to economic fears and repercussions accompanying the beginning of World War I.

March 5, 1933 proved its most skittish day when President Franklin Roosevelt abruptly declared a local bank holiday directly affecting the Exchange and Mellon Financial and PNC Banks.

A long-term solution towards the institution's future was explored during the 1960s. On December 24, 1969, the Philadelphia-Baltimore-Washington DC Stock Exchange purchased the Pittsburgh entity. Their intention included keeping the trading floor open.

The number of exchange members increasingly dwindled. From its former apex of 1,200 companies, only 11 companies traded shares on the final official trading day, August 23, 1974. The exchange office closed its 333 Fourth Avenue headquarters upon consolidating trades with the Chicago, New York and various global exchanges.

Once the stock exchange vacated the building, two nightclubs occupied the premises. In 2006, Point Park University purchased the building. They converted the interior into office space.

**A Kennywood Park Landmark Destroyed and Forgotten
In Nearly A Single Day
Kennywood Amusement Park:
4800 Kennywood Boulevard, West Mifflin**

The afternoon of June 19, 1975 reached scorching 90+ degree temperatures in Pittsburgh. The suburban Kennywood amusement park had recently installed a new water ride called the *Log Jammer*. The ride had required ten months to construct, but offered the ultimate repose for a summer's heatwave. Riders were guaranteed to exit soaked.

The park that day was packed. During the afternoon, a relic of generations past, the *Pavilion*, would command preeminent attention. The site was once known as the former Kennywood Dance Hall. The building had evolved into a secondary shaded ride called the *Ghost Ship*. It was one of the first structures constructed in the park when it opened in 1898. The two-story building had covered windows and rugged but exposed wooden beams.

During the Great Depression and Big Band Era, the *Pavilion* hosted live performances of nationally renowned bandleaders and singers. Dancing was popular, but smoking and alcohol strictly forbidden.

The introduction of television slackened the interest towards live dance venues. Park management converted the building into a succession of rides.

On July 19th, a park assistant manager detected smoke in the rear of the *Ghost Ship*. Ride workers promptly evacuated individuals inside. A fire alarm was sounded. Kennywood workers streamed toward the ride with fire extinguishers and hoses. The building's ancient wood became ideal kindling. Soon flames engulfed the structure and would spread to two additional rides in the *Kiddieland* section, the *Kiddie Whip* and *Merry-go-round*.

Fire departments from the region expediently arrived and extinguished the blaze. The park, despite the drama, remained open. An estimated 2,000 visitors viewed the battle for containment in the unbearable heat. The firefighting effort doused the fire by 3:00 p.m. The *Pavilion* was damaged beyond saving. There were no human casualties with the exception of one Duquesne firefighter overcome by the heat. He was transferred to McKeesport Hospital and later released.

Within days, the wreckage had been cleared and re-landscaped with freshly planted grass. The park continued ongoing operations as though completely unaffected by the loss. By the following year, the space would be converted into a plaza featuring a fountain and new entrance to *Kiddieland*. All trace of the former landmark and its memories had been forgotten.

Detonation of a Pitt University Study Center
Langley Hall: 171 Tennyson Street, Pittsburgh

At approximately 12:40 p.m. on January 20, 1977, the University of Pittsburgh's Langley Hall detonated from an explosion caused by a natural gas leak. An estimated 160 students were attending a Physiology class in one of the lecture halls adjacent to the blast site. Glass windows more than 75 feet away were blown out and other campus buildings within the vicinity were shaken.

Two individuals were killed and 47 others injured as the explosion ripped open the structure and collapsed a portion of its roof. The unfortunate two were Carleen Curry, a department secretary and Patricia Hostetler, chemistry major.

Curry was on the telephone with a member of her family when the blast erupted killing her instantly. Hostetler had just kissed her boyfriend moments before. Both became trapped by the collapsed roof and falling debris. He suffered multiple fractures in his back but would be rescued and later recover.

The sole warning for the disaster was a detected foul odor permeating the premises.

The timing could have been even worse as a psychology class of 200 students had just been let out of the lecture hall ten minutes before. Their classroom was located immediately above the center of the explosion. Five years would pass before Langley Hall could be completely rebuilt. The building was reopened in 1982.

UNIVERSITY OF PITTSBURGH
LANGLEY HALL

A Pornography Lord Silenced In An Alleyway
Maddock Place, Pittsburgh

The February 25, 1977 murder of Pittsburgh pornography king George E. Lee did not stimulate great police enthusiastic for apprehending his killers. Many viewed the act as trash cleaning up its own. Two men accosted Lee in an alleyway at 11:30 p.m. between 7th and 8th Streets near Fort Duquesne Boulevard. They had been anticipating his appearance.

The pair wasted no time in shooting him in the head and chest. Lee had just finished dinner and was heading towards his bronze-colored Cadillac. The contract killers had left no option for his potential escape as they'd flattened his front tire. After the shooting, they entered their own red and white Chevrolet and raced away from the scene.

Police considered Lee, 57, a notable vice lord of downtown Pittsburgh. He owned and operated *Studio One*, a Ninth Street massage parlor. He was also known as a business partner with Anthony *Ninny* Laggatutta.

Laggatutta was incarcerated at the time of the murder based on evidence implicating him of a downtown commercial arson fire. He was scheduled the following week to stand trial for the beating death of a lawyer in January 1976. Lee had been subpoenaed to testify at his partner's inquest, but police couldn't locate him.

Lee had an extended history of criminal activity including operating a house of prostitution. He had ownership stakes in porno shops, X-rated movie theatres, after-hours clubs and additional massage parlors. A week before his death, police had raided a warehouse that FBI agents considered the main supplier for pornography businesses in the region. Lee had been rumored to be an owner.

Over time, the investigation grew frigid due to the absence of cooperation with his associates. Lee simply became a forgotten underworld anecdote. His killers and the motive behind his death would never be publicly identified.

A Haunting Leg Amputation of a Bridge Worker Replacement Span: Birmingham Bridge, Pittsburgh

Journeyman ironworker Ralph Winner Jr. would never forget May 22, 1978 or Pittsburgh's Brady Street Bridge. The span had outlived its usefulness and was scheduled to be detonated into the Monongahela River.

The steel bowstring arch bridge had opened in 1896. Two lanes of traffic were accommodated between Brady Street on the Pittsburgh side and South 22nd Street on the south side. Approach viaducts were built at each end.

The bridge was officially closed on May 3, 1976. The opening of its replacement, the Birmingham Bridge wouldn't begin until the summer of 1977.

The date set for the Brady Bridge's demolition was May 29, 1978. A week prior towards noon, workers were making welding cuts into the bridge to hold explosive charges. Ralph Winner made a cut on his side of the bridge. A girder shifted and a heavy steel plate pinned both of his legs.

For over two hours, six men attempted to cut him free. They were able to cut around the plate to extricate his left leg. They determined a subsequent cut of the plate around his right leg risked causing the bridge to give way. Dr. Joseph C. Young, a surgeon was called in to complete a horrific procedure. He needed to saw off Winner's right leg to release the rest of his body.

The amputation was performed in drizzling rain as Young was perched atop the 127-foot-high bridge. Winner was given morphine and intravenous solutions to prevent him from going into shock during the operation. The drugs assisted with some pain management, but didn't relieve the agony of what was to follow.

From the neighboring Birmingham Bridge, traffic had slowed to a standstill. Over 200 spectators viewed the horror from there. Winner's screams were audible throughout the operation. He was transported afterwards to Presbyterian University Hospital where he would recover.

Winner's ironworker career ended that day, but he became admired for motivating other amputees to live on with life. He continued doing odd construction and handiwork tasks. He would die in April 2016 at the age of 87, surviving his wife of 57 years and two siblings.

A Snowplower's Laced Whiskey Poisoning
McKees Rocks Streets and Sanitation Department:
1385 Island Avenue, McKees Rocks

McKees Rocks Streets Commissioner Jimmy Goodnight was considered a very fortunate convicted felon. His shadowy past stemmed from a 1971 conviction over hijacking $20,000 in gourmet cheese being transported between Baltimore and Chicago. He served three years for the crime. At the age of 47, he rebounded with the esteemed Commissioner position.

On the evening of January 4, 1979, he supervised the salting and cindering of local roads prior to the arrival an approaching snowstorm. He returned to his office and poured a glass from his whiskey bottle inventory. The source of this bottle was never determined. Appreciative residents commonly distributed liquor to snowplowers.

Goodnight indulged briefly and then abruptly dropped to the floor. The content was laced with enough cyanide to kill 30 people. His death was instantaneous.

Prior to the autopsy, his demise was suspected to be a heart attack. The results confirmed poisoning. Rumors circulated that his murder was prompted by a gambling debt to an impatient creditor.

Suburban McKees Rocks would return to the headlines in July 1987 with the beating and strangulation of retired local policeman Marty Fitzpatrick. The killing was particularly vicious and personal. Fitzpatrick was attacked and robbed after leaving a social club and gambling party. He was tied to the bumper of a car and dragged several blocks.

Suspicious deaths arrived in threes. In October 1988, Bobby Mancini became outed as a police informant. He was shot to death inside his apartment shortly afterwards.

All three of the killings remain unsolved, but have a suspected linkage to Mafia associate Alolpho *Junior* Williams. Williams owned the social club that Fitzpatrick had left before his murder and was influential in McKees Rocks' illicit activities. He would never be tried on those suspicions. Williams would die of a heart attack in April 2016 leaving his culpability a question of speculation.

**Levity in the Court of Common Pleas
Allegheny County Common Pleas Court:
414 Grant Street, Pittsburgh**

The Allegheny County Court of Common Pleas is one of 60 judicial courts within Pennsylvania designated to hear major civil and criminal cases. Since the building's opening in 1884, the emphasis remains on *serious* trials. Levity has been known to clandestinely intrude.

In the late 1980s, a Pittsburgh attorney was scheduled to defend a client inside a magistrate's office. He was appearing before both an unsympathetic judge and police officer that had filed the case. They had conspired to cite the attorney for driving without a license upon his appearance. At that time, it was known that he did not possess a valid license. A professional peer overheard the intentioned trap and warned his colleague. The defending attorney arrived to his appointment punctual, but with a twist. He arrived on horseback and tied his ride to a tree just outside of the judge's office.

In 1989, a criminal defense attorney was concluding his final arguments before a jury and flailing directionless. The county prosecutor felt confident that her case was proceeding well and a conviction eminent. It was her initial year in the position and she knew her court adversary only by reputation. In mid argument, the defense attorney's briefcase began to ring. In 1989, cell phones were awkwardly oversized and extremely rare. For owners, they became a prestige accompaniment.

The defense attorney apologized to the judge and courtroom. He proceeded to not only answer, but also complete the call. The impression mesmerized the jury according to the prosecutor. They acquitted his client after only thirty minutes of deliberation.

One year before his death in 2002, Judge Robert Dauer decided to dress as wizard Harry Potter for Halloween. The following year, Judge David Cashman decided that he'd dress in a wizard's costume on the same occasion in honor of his deceased colleague. He accessorized with a powder blue robe and a pointy hat adorned with white stars.

One of his defendants appearing that day was a perpetrator cited previously for driving under the influence. At their first encounter, Cashman had consigned him to the Mayview State Hospital for psychiatric evaluation. This appearance was a follow-up to that evaluation.

When the defendant appeared before the judge who was wearing his wizard outfit, he questioned immediately who was the saner between the two. He asked the judge who he was supposed to be.

The judge responded *I'm a wizard.*

Where's your wand?

I don't have a wand, but I have a fountain pen.

How are you supposed to make me disappear with that?

Judge Cashman concluded with a smile. *Over the years, I have made more people disappear with this pen than you know.*

Cashman found the defendant guilty.

Pennsylvania's 666 Lottery Scam
WTAE Television Station:
400 Ardmore Boulevard, Pittsburgh

Nick Perry (real name Nicholas Katsafanas) epitomized Pittsburgh media integrity and stability during the 1970s. Perry was raised locally, attended Duquesne University and served in the U.S. Navy during World War II. Following his military service, he began a radio broadcasting career in Charleston, West Virginia. He next advanced over to Pittsburgh television station WDTV. In 1958, he switched over to rival WTAE to become a staff announcer.

At WTAE, he became a news and weather reporter and hosted *Bowling For Dollars* and *Championship Bowling*. His greatest visibility arrived in 1977 when he became the host of the nightly broadcast for the Pennsylvania Lottery staged inside WTAE's studios.

Lottery odds are historically long. The probability of selecting the correct sequence is theoretically impossible to predict. Perry along with two partners from a side vending machine business determined that by rigging the number of possible outcomes, success became nearly guaranteed.

At the time, numbered ping-pong balls inside a machine determined the lottery. Perry arranged a WTAE art director to create weighted replicas of the ping-pong balls. The number 4 and 6 balls were chosen as designated *lighter* balls from the rest. With only these two numbers probable to show up, the winning sequence was limited to eight possible combinations.

Perry was one of two individuals with key access to both the lottery machine and the ping-pong balls. He enabled a WTAE stagehand to physically switch the customary balls with the replicas before a specific drawing.

On April 24, 1980, the jackpot had reached a record payoff of $3.5 million. Perry's group of co-conspirators accumulated large quantities of tickets throughout Pennsylvania with one of the eight possible combinations. That evening, the winning number sequence was 666. Six million statewide viewers watched the outcome. Eight winners materialized to split the proceeds.

Immediately following the telecast, the same WTAE stagehand removed the doctored ping-pong balls from the machine. He replacing them with the customary batch that he'd switched earlier. The replica balls were immediately incinerated inside a paint can. The perfect heist appeared undetectable.

Lottery officials became immediately suspicious by the volume of winners and tickets purchased targeting the eight possible outcomes.

One bar owner in Philadelphia fingered a significant purchase made by two brothers and a platinum-blonde woman for solely those numbers.

As a conspiracy became evident, participating rats floated towards the surface. Some implicated their partners-in-crime receiving lighter sentences. Seven individuals would be charged with the focus and prime target being broadcaster Nick Perry.

Most of the winning allocations would be recovered. In May 1981, Nick Perry would be convicted of criminal conspiracy, criminal mischief, theft by deception, rigging a publicly exhibited contest and perjury. He was sentenced to seven years of incarceration and remained on parole until March 1989.

Upon his release, his legacy was forever tarnished due to the scandal. He attempted an unsuccessful return to broadcasting towards the end of the decade. Afterwards, he would disappear from public visibility. He died in Massachusetts at the age of 87 in 2003.

He would never admit to any role in the plot.

Serial Killer Sidney Brinkley Redistributes His Childhood Agony
Murder Site: Litchfield Towers, Fourth Floor, University of Pittsburgh
4200 Fifth Avenue, Pittsburgh

By the time Philadelphia construction worker Sidney Brinkley was put on trial for the murder of coed Monica Jones, he had already been sentenced to three life terms for other killings.

One might conceivably feel empathy for Brinkley. His mother Bessie Grace admitted that she had *occasionally* beaten her son while he was growing up. She even admitted to once tying his feet and hands to a bed and beating him with an electric cord until he bled. Brinkley carried the mental and physical scars of that senseless attempt at discipline.

With such an abusive background, a life of debauchery and abuse towards women seemed almost inevitable. At no stage could it become a rationale or justification for his later violence and behavior.

Profiles regarding Sidney Brinkley identified him as either 22 or 26-years-old. On January 4, 1979, he fatally assaulted Monica Jones. The 18-year-old was raised in North Philadelphia. She was a pre-med student attending the University of Pittsburgh. She lived on the fourth floor of Litchfield Towers, a school dormitory. She was a friend of Brinkley's then girlfriend.

While his girlfriend waited for him sitting in a car, Brinkley launched into his attack. His girlfriend testified that she was completely unaware of his activities. Brinkley tortured Jones, raped her twice and then choked and strangled her to death. He slid her body down the fourth floor laundry chute. She would be discovered later in the collecting receptacle of the basement trash room.

So heinous was his violation of Jones, that the death penalty became an immediate consideration as punishment. Jones was convicted for the murder in October 1981. His jury wavered over a life sentence or capital punishment. Four separate votes did not resolve the issue. Each time they voted, they were unaware of his three prior murders and consecutive life sentences.

Serial killer Brinkley eventually receded from the headlines. His name is no longer published on the Pennsylvania Department of Corrections inventory of prisoners.

Abhorrent parenting contributed towards the monster that became Sidney Brinkley. He merely redistributed his private hell to at least four innocent women. His parents would never be held accountable as being his impetus.

Litchfield Towers

The Startling Identity of the 1980 Hat Bandit
Dollar Bank Aborted Robbery Site:
6047 US-30, Greensburg

Gene Miller boasted an impressive professional pedigree. He had earned a degree from Dartmouth College, served in the military, was an executive for JC Penney and ultimately became the editor at the *Mt. Pleasant Journal*, *Jeannette News-Dispatch* and *The Spark*.

He was acknowledged as an intelligent, respectable individual in Mt. Pleasant, known for his quick wit, motivational abilities and eccentric sport coats.

His most enduring identity however resulted in 1980 when he was identified and arrested as being the notorious *Hat Bandit*. Over a two-year, three county bank robbery spree, he reportedly stole $44,500 from eleven banks.

Miller employed various disguises during each crime. His fake mustaches coupled by fedora and bucket hats distinguished him. Bank surveillance photos were circulated publicly by police, but failed to identify him.

Instead his carelessness while casing another attempted robbery would result in his downfall. State Police Sgt. Thomas Tridico was patrolling banks between Pleasant Unity and Hempfield during December 1980. Miller began acting suspiciously outside of a Dollar Savings Bank in Hempfield nearing 11:00 a.m. Miller's car had a cardboard license plate and he continued to drive around the parking lot repeatedly.

After exhaustively scanning and comparing the surveillance photos of the *Hat Bandit*, Tridico arrested Miller at 12:40 p.m. Federal authorities would connect Miller to the previous robberies. His trial judge called the spree one of the most *brilliantly executed* he had seen.

Miller pleaded guilty and was sentenced in June 1981 to 20 years in federal prison. He would be released three years later, possibly due to his exemplary reputation within the community. Upon his release, he disappeared completely from public view. He died at the age of 89 in Hempfield on May 24, 2017.

His former press employees universally praised his character and concern regarding the ethics of the newspaper. According to them, he genuinely cared about the paper's quality regardless of his own lack of financial compensation.

Perhaps he could simply compartmentalize journalistic ethics with his materialistic desires and greed. Like renowned bank robber Willie Sutton once responded when asked why he robbed banks. He flatly stated *because that's where the money is*.

An Unsolved Multi-Million Dollar St. Patrick Day Heist
Former Purolator Armored Car Terminal
2728 Lachman Way, Brentwood

Towards the end of St. Patrick's Day 1982, security guard James Powers was in the middle of his graveyard shift. He was working alone that evening. Powers patrolled a Purolator company armored truck terminal in Brentwood, a southern borough of Metropolitan Pittsburgh.

Nearing 11:30 p.m., two men ducked under a rear garage door as a truck exited the depot to make a delivery. The pair wore trench coats, dark felt hats and Aviator sunglasses. One was white and the other black. Each was approximately 6 feet tall. Both carried a walkie-talkie as they approached the guard. They explained that they were FBI agents anticipating a potential robbery at the facility that evening.

Their appearance seemed genuine and both flashed facsimile credentials. Powers had little initial reason to doubt their credibility.

The two men abruptly overpowered and disarmed him of his shotgun and pistol. He was handcuffed, tied up and had his mouth and eyes taped over. He was escorted to an employee lounge where he was obliged to lie on the floor. He was not physically harmed.

With practiced precision, the pair removed the guard's keys to access a vault area. Awaiting their entry were 26 bags filled with cash destined for distribution to western Pennsylvania banks. Since time was tenuous and the arrival of additional delivery trucks possible, the pair efficiently transferred the sacks via metal carts to an awaiting vehicle outside. Published accounts indicated that over five hundred pounds of cash were stolen valued at $2.5 million.

Powers eventually discarded the tape covering his mouth and was able to notify a third party to telephone police. By 1:00 a.m. the Purolator terminal was inundated with law enforcement officers. The robbers' vehicle had long vanished into the pitch dark. The crime scene revealed no substantial clues.

FBI investigators suspected that Powers was complicit in the theft being the only other witness on site. The stealth and timing of the theft made him an obvious *inside* participant. The suspicion regarding his involvement could never be proven. He denied participation, but would still be fired by Purolator one month later. He died in 1996 leaving the solitary known linkage to the crime missing.

The investigation following the theft traced a circuitous trail that went nowhere. Suspects included a Pittsburgh police officer who'd resigned just a few days previously. No one talked, saw anything or appeared to know any intimate details. Less than two years following the robbery, Purolator would sell its armored car operation to an Australian firm and who later closed the facility.

The case remains perpetually cold. Certain local criminals would be speculated upon as possible participants. None were ever indicted for the theft.

The most compelling suspect that emerged eight years later was mobster Geno Chiarelli. He was publicly outed as a person of interest in the 1985 disappearance of associate Joseph Bertone concerning a drug proceeds dispute. Bertone's Cadillac Seville was discovered abandoned in the parking lot of a Holiday Inn. His body was never recovered.

Between March 7-9, 1986, Chiarelli was instrumental in a vault heist at the First Seneca Bank of Greensburg with three other men. He would turn himself in following a narrow escape from police in Tampa, Florida in December 1987. His crew was attempting to fence some of the stolen items from the theft.

He was indicted the following month and ultimately found guilty on three counts of transferring stolen property. His 40-month sentence in federal prison was compounded in April 1990 by a more expansive indictment involving nine perpetrators on racketeering and corruption charges.

At his September 1990 trial, a low-level cocaine distributor testified that Chiarelli had confessed to him of orchestrating the Purolator robbery. The distributor's legitimacy was largely dismissed based on a suspicion of revenge as his motive. Chiarelli would be convicted of racketeering and drug trafficking and sentenced to 22 years in prison. He would be released in 2008 and die four years later.

Periodically, accounts of the theft circulate via newspaper articles or crime blogs. The statute of limitations for the crime has expired. The terminal has been repurposed. The criminal leaders that composed the once feared Pittsburgh mob are deceased.

A fascination over an unsolved robbery of such magnitude remains. The cash will never be recovered. The individuals that do know the truth had the discretion to keep their knowledgeable circle small.

A Fatal Fall and Momentary Pause For Reflection and Priority

University of Pittsburgh Brackenridge Hall, 3rd Floor: 3990 Fifth Avenue, Pittsburgh

During the late evening before the University of Pittsburgh's football team's next day departure to the 1983 Cotton Bowl, harsh reality intervened. Todd Becker, 20, a sophomore linebacker from Massachusetts was attempting to evade trouble. Instead he forfeited his life out of careless judgment.

Becker had issues with alcohol and restraint. His enabling friends, peers and acquaintances did little to address these problems until they no longer could. On Thursday evening, December 16, 1982, Becker entered a third-story window of Brackenridge Hall, a campus dormitory aided by easy access on one side of the building.

He was a familiar face to security personnel because he'd become unwelcome from attending dormitory functions. He'd been banned due to several accumulating infractions that he'd committed when he'd lived in Brackenridge the previous year.

Becker attended a sixth floor party and proceeded to become inebriated. His blood alcohol content was 0.15, twice the legal limit of intoxication. Passing midnight, Becker suddenly panicked because he thought that he'd been seen by security inside the dorm. He feared that being caught would prevent him from playing in the impending Cotton Bowl.

He returned to his former entry window only to discover that the room where it was located had since been locked. He hastily attempted to exit from another third-floor window unaware of his bearings. He miscalculated the height from the ground. He had planned to lower himself to the ground from a ledge that he assumed was located below the window. The ledge didn't exist. Instead he fell to his death in a freak accident.

Becker was transferred immediately to the emergency room of Presbyterian-University Hospital. His coach arrived shortly after 2 a.m. to learn that he'd expired from his injuries.

The team's departure for Dallas that evening would be delayed for Becker's memorial service. Commonly college teams arrived two weeks before the January 1st scheduled contest to enable adequate preparation time.

The 1983 Cotton Bowl featured an anticipated showdown between Pitt's heralded quarterback Dan Marino and Southwestern Methodist University (SMU)'s running back Eric Dickerson. Both players would become professional first round draft picks and eventual Hall of Famers.

The contest proved to be a dud with the final score 7-3 won by SMU. There is little doubt the shadow of Becker's death influenced Pitt players' performances. In 1987, the NCAA would shut down the SMU football program for excessive rules violations.

Following Becker's death, football fleetingly appeared marginalized in priority. For that abbreviated instant, the necessity to drink without restraint likewise appeared superficial and unnecessary.

Neither sentiment would remain sustained.

**A Crumbling Memorial For The Disenfranchised
Immaculate Heart of Mary Church School
3029 Paulowna Street, Pittsburgh**

Polish Hill is a distinctive ethnic center wedged amidst the Strip, Lower Lawrenceville and Upper Hill districts. The neighborhood was formerly known as Herron Hill before a mass arrival of Polish immigrants during the 1890s prompted a name change.

In 1895, permission was granted for the construction of a worship building that combined church services, a school and convent. The cornerstone was laid in October 1896 and still remains embedded. The multi-level red brick building was competed the following year.

Initially, the first level served as a school, while church services were conducted on the second floor. In 1899, the parish purchased land below for a larger basilica that has become known as the accompanying Immaculate Heart of Mary Church. The church officially was dedicated for service on December 3, 1905. Its most compelling aspect is an enormous aesthetically striking dome. The dome is painted mint green, resembling natural copper patina.

The dome has evolved into a treasured icon for both the Diocese of Pittsburgh and the city. In July 2013, a fierce electrical storm struck the dome directly causing visible smoke and a fire. Fifteen firemen mounted the structure until the top to expediently extinguish the blaze.

The church has prospered for over a century. The original brick school behind eventually graduated its final class in 1987. The structure has since languished in decay. Efforts to refurbish and/or repurpose the building have met city planning resistance and disapproval due to the existing presence of lead, asbestos and suspected foundation deterioration.

Since the school's closure, an alternative community has frequently and visibly occupied the premises. Squatters habitually entered through the second level and left personal forms of defacement, graffiti and messages on both the interior and exterior.

Outside, spray painted stenciled memorials freeze time. A morbid fascination is stimulated to know whether these stenciled individuals actually existed and what was the accompanying narrative behind their life and premature death.

This same imagery along with tagged graffiti scrawls equally provokes revulsion that once beautiful architecture could be so thoughtlessly vandalized and damaged.

As the year's pass and the damages accumulate, a most likely outcome will become demolition. In the meantime, the building serves as a layered canvas for the disenfranchised seeking a medium of expression that conventional society has legally denied them.

SCHOLA POLONICA
IMM CORDIS M.
A. 1896 D

Francesca
Araya
Rest In
Punk
1988
2018

A Detached Bell Tower Remains Via Compromise
Bellefield Tower:
Corner Fifth and Bellefield Avenue, Pittsburgh

Bellefield Tower is the final compromise and remnant of a church that once occupied a distinctive Oakland neighborhood corner. The tower is a lingering portion of the Bellefield Presbyterian Church built on former pastureland. Neville Craig, editor of the *Pittsburgh Gazette* between 1829-1841, once owned the site.

The entire Gothic Revival structure was completed in 1889 and designed by local architect Frederick Osterling, renowned for the Union Trust Building downtown. The sandstone and mortar composition features intricate detailing and carvings.

Seven years following completion on a Thackeray Avenue location, the First United Presbyterian Church was constructed. The nearby addition accommodated a downtown based congregation. For decades, the two churches co-existed, divided by minor denominational differences.

In 1967, the Pittsburgh Presbytery, a regional governing body, decided to merge the congregations. As the First United structure was in better condition, it was allowed to remain. The Bellefield Avenue structure became no longer necessary and was sold in the 1980s to the University of Pittsburgh.

Shortly afterwards, the National Development Corporation decided to build an office complex on the Bellefield church site. An immediate public uproar prompted a concession in the design of the proposed sleek office. The architects were able to preserve the church's corner tower while demolishing the remainder of the edifice.

Conditions publicized in March 1985 stipulated that the tower would neither be functional or open to the public. The bell would also be removed.

The compromise structure currently shades an adjacent diminutive courtyard. The sight of the detached tower is a reminder of the building's past historical significance. It is likewise a viewing oddity for those unaware of the accompanying historical narrative.

Fencing Unsalable Stolen Treasures
First Seneca Bank:
19 North Main Street, Greensburg

Over the course of the March 8, 1986 weekend, burglars drilled several large holes in the ceiling of the First Seneca Bank located in Greensburg. Eventually accessing the bank's vault, the crew reportedly stole $80,000 in cash along with sixteen antique Renaissance weapons from a safe deposit box. The entirety of stolen assets was never publicly itemized.

The ornate, pearl, ivory and gold inlaid weapons dated from the 15th to 17th century. Collectively they were appraised between $1-$2 million. Amongst the inventory were several wheel-lock pistols and an Augsburg hunting sword.

Stealing such extravagant treasures proved an exceptional coup. Profiting from the theft and finding a potential purchasing outlet became impossible. Ironically, the insurance policy underwriter, Aetna Insurance, became the only interested party for resale. The adjusters assigned to process the insurance claim contacted a criminal third party to negotiate the delicate re-purchase. This intermediary was George *Sonny* Jordan.

Concluding a year of negotiations, Aetna offered $385,000. The thieves eventually accepted the terms. The actual burglars were never conclusively identified. Jordan had informally confessed to an Aetna representative that the split of the proceeds would involve eight parties.

The presumed burglars were career criminals Geno Chiarelli, Arleigh Halterman and Anthony Durich. All three men would become directly involved in the transfer of the stolen merchandise to Aetna.

Once the negotiations were concluded, arrangements were made to meet in Tampa, Florida on December 15, 1987.

The thieves erroneously presumed this would be a private transaction without law enforcement intervention. The FBI was secretly and intimately involved in the negotiations and had crafted a surveillance and apprehension strategy.

Chiarelli, Halterman, Durich and Jordan arrived in Tampa on December 13, 1987. FBI agents tailed their movements. The criminals cautiously employed two vehicles, a rented Buick car and grey Chevrolet van. They communicated between the vehicles via two-way hand held radios. They also employed two radio scanners capable of monitoring radio frequencies used by law enforcement agencies.

The group stayed at a nondescript Clearwater Beach motel on the evening of December 14th. The next day they established with the buyer representatives a transfer destination and time. A downtown Tampa shopping mall parking lot was agreed upon. The criminal foursome carefully plotted their movements and employed elusive driving strategies under the watchful eye of FBI monitoring.

Prior to the actual exchange, FBI agents observed the transfer of a green duffel bag from the van to the car. Operating on the assumption that the bag contained the stolen weaponry, agents approached the Buick and detained Durish and Jordan. They recovered the duffel bag inside a locked trunk. They would not inspect the contents until days later when they'd secured a legal search warrant.

Halterman and Chiarelli viewed the arrests from inside their nearby parked van and sped away. Halterman was the driver and exited the parking lot via a sidewalk nearly striking an agent's car. He then crossed into oncoming traffic accelerating to speeds of eighty miles per hour. He entered a residential neighborhood and swerved around a school bus unloading children. Due to the danger to vehicles and pedestrians imposed by his reckless driving, he temporarily evaded pursuit.

He was sighted ten minutes later in downtown Tampa and agents resumed the chase. He was finally trapped inside a sealed off street and arrested. Chiarelli was no longer his passenger and a search that afternoon for him proved fruitless. Two days later he would voluntarily surrender at the FBI office in Pittsburgh.

At trial, all four participants were indicted for the possession and transportation of stolen property. Jordan would die on May 5, 1988 from an unrelated auto accident resulting in the dismissal of charges against him. The three remaining men's 1989 convictions resulted in modest prison sentences. Chiarelli received the harshest of 40 months.

Chiarelli was considered a ranking member of Pittsburgh's LaRocca crime family. He had been involved intimately in large-scale cocaine trafficking, extortion, and robbery. A carpenter by trade, he'd developed a reputation for his proficiency with safes and vaults.

His name would be prominently attached to various Pittsburgh misdeeds. His first public exposure originated with the operation and 1972 suspicious closing of the *Showboat Club*, a local mob nightspot. He engineered an arson fire that destroyed one of his prohibitively insured residences. He was suspected of being involved in the unsolved 1982 Purolator armored car terminal theft and disappearance and presumed murder of associate Joseph Bertone.

He spent the majority of his declining years incarcerated following a federal investigation and conviction. Four years following his release in 2008, he died of lung cancer at the age of 69.

Despite the criminal's presumed guilt in the First Seneca Bank heist, none of them would be arrested for the crime. Burglary charges were never filed.

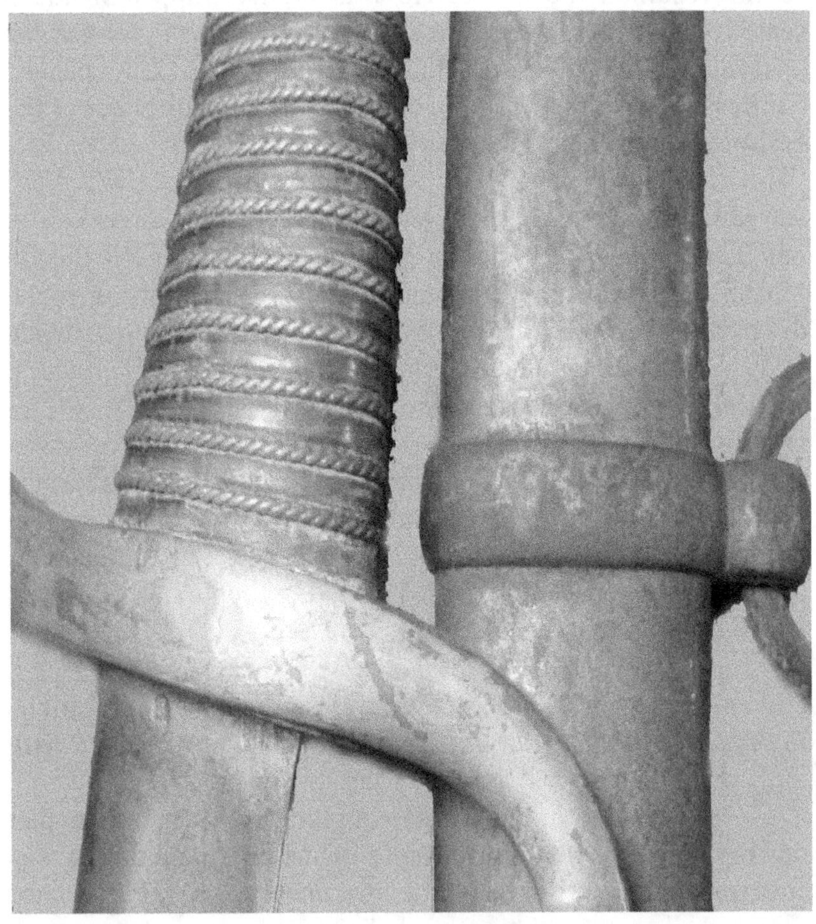

A Hometown Renowned Artist and His Enduring Legacy
Andy Warhol Museum:
117 Sandusky Street, Pittsburgh
Andy Warhol Bridge (Seventh Street Bridge), Pittsburgh
Grave: St. John the Baptist Byzantine Catholic Cemetery
1066 Connor Road, Pittsburgh

Andy Warhol (born Warhola) was born in Pittsburgh in 1928. He graduated from Schenley High School at sixteen and earned his bachelor's degree in pictorial design from the Carnegie Institute of Technology. His Pittsburgh formation remained an anchoring influence throughout his New York City based visual art career and global acclaim.

The Pittsburgh that Warhol knew during the 1940s was blackened by smoke and pollution originating from the steel mills. Warhol's family resided in a succession of local neighborhoods near the smokestacks along the Monongahela River. Streetlights were often turned on during daylight hours due to the density of the smog.

Warhol's audience and future was destined for more cosmopolitan, progressive and edgy tastes. Provincial Pittsburgh would have blunted his prospects. He opted to seek his fortune and distinctive vision within New York City. He created a production center called *The Factory* venturing into additional medias including music, publishing and film. Once installed, his creativity lunged forward never scanning a mirror backwards.

His family and Pittsburgh years etched an enduring legacy into his conflictive and perceived hedonistic character. His mother was a devout Catholic whose beliefs and habits were transferred to him. Throughout his New York residence and travels, Warhol habitually attended daily mass and carried a rosary in his pocket.

Warhol's earliest sketches framed an embedded memory of the Pittsburgh he adored from arms distance. One of his favorite drawing locations was near the site that would become the future Andy Warhol Museum.

Warhol throughout his life hedged in interviews on the legitimacy of his originality. Many art critics praised him for his adaptation of contemporary design tools such as screen-printing rather than the novelty of his ideas. Part of his attraction is that his imagery was accessible and simplistic to interpret. His output blurred the traditional boundaries between highbrow and common consumer tastes. He didn't bother to distinguish the difference.

He was a superb marketer that comprehended strategic placement of his work. He understood that maintaining your production in high profile collections, exhibitions, auction houses and museums far exceeded subjective genius. He heightened his visibility by courting controversy with shocking conceptual themes or framing celebrities from a distinct perspective.

His visibility within the art world and relationship with publishing patriarchs maintained his *relevancy*.

There remains a debate as to whether he belongs within the pantheon of great artists. Selling prices of his work often dominate the discussion, but remain distant criteria from actual talent and longevity.

Warhol died abruptly on February 22, 1987 from complications following a routine gallbladder operation. He was 58-years-old and his funeral was attended by only close confidants. His unforeseen departure preventing his legacy from over scrupulous examination and possible long-term decline. Exhibitions of his work remain globally popular and well attended.

Pittsburgh generously honored its native son with an art museum bearing his name. His career is also acknowledged by the renaming of the former Seventh Avenue Bridge after him. He is buried locally at the St. John the Baptist Byzantine Catholic Cemetery.

**An Incestuous Murder For A Previous Prison Lifer
Clinton Apartments: 283 Moon Clinton Road, Moon**

On April 7, 1972, Gary Lee Starr shot his wife Linda to death in Rochester, Pennsylvania. His defense at the time was that she'd cheated on him. Despite receiving a life imprisonment sentence, he would only serve 8 1/2 years for the murder. The consequences of the killing left him both a widower and the father of a daughter, Wanda.

Upon his release, the pair developed a corrupted relationship that evolved into incest by the time she was fourteen. During the next six years, their bond deepened into an unhealthy co-dependence.
Wanda would reportedly *manipulate him through sexual promises*.

Gary Starr remarried, but kept his illicit relationship secret for obvious reasons. Wanda had borne him a son in 1985. Starr was employed as a custodian and rent collector at an apartment complex. He invited her to live there in a separate unit. She began dating and ultimately living with a man two years older than her in late January 1988. In mid March, they decided to marry. He was unaware of who was the father of her son.

Gary Lee Starr had sustained a controlling influence on his daughter. He felt that her impending fiancé was *irresponsible*. He claimed that he did want her to marry, perhaps hoping the past might continue to remain camouflaged.

Their deception became revealed on February 20, 1988. Father and daughter fought viciously. He accused her of stealing rent money and threatened to inform her fiancé regarding their past. Wanda countered by threatening to expose him to his current wife.

The screaming between them escalated out of control. Gary Starr grabbed a knife and stabbed Wanda 35 times to death. Her bloodied body would be discovered later inside her apartment by her fiancé.

The sordid details would be published publicly. Gary Starr concocted a story that he'd *blacked out* just before the murder. He apparently thought his tact might absolve him from homicide. Starr pled guilty during his two-day trial in August 1988 to first-degree murder and was sentenced to death.

On appeal in 1995, his conviction was reversed and a new trial conducted. The reversal was based on the original court's refusal to allow Starr to act as his own counsel and revoke his earlier guilty plea.

On January 12, 1996, Starr pleaded guilty once again to first-degree murder and was resentenced to life imprisonment. He is currently interned at the SCI Laurel Highlands Institution in Somerset. The then two-year old son that he and his daughter had together was placed in a foster home.

The Shuffled Fortunes of A Pittsburgh Bread Institution
Former Braun Baking Company Location:
1700 Island Avenue, Pittsburgh

Baby Boomers growing up in Western Pennsylvania during the 1950s and 60s were intimately familiar with the orange-and-yellow striped bags of *Town Talk* bread on grocery store shelves. During that era, the brand was produced at Pittsburgh's Braun Baking Company that originally opened operations in 1889.

In 1958, Continental Baking Company of New York bought Braun Baking following the death of owner E. R. Braun. In 1968, International Telephone and Telegraph would acquire Continental Baking. The Ralston Purina Corporation of St. Louis would subsequently acquire the Continental brand in 1984.

Continental would shutter the North Side Braun facility in May 1989 resulting in the loss of 110 jobs. Production would be relocated to Philadelphia.

Three years later, former Braun workers founded employee owned City Pride Bakery in the Lawrenceville Industrial Park.

The promise of employee owned success withered within a year. In desperation, convicted con man Michael Carlow and his Pittsburgh Food and Beverage Company were given management control. Carlow managed to lose and siphon off $4 million during an eleven-month period. City Pride Bakery was forced to close in February 1994 resulting in 177 lost jobs.

In 1995, Interstate Bakeries Corporation of Kansas City bought Continental Baking from Ralston Purina and established production of *Town Talk* to an Akron, Ohio plant.

In 2005, they began to phase out the brand modifying the packaging to include the more familiar national Wonder Bread label. Their marketing strategy was to continue selling exclusively in the Pittsburgh market and monitor the results. In 2009, Continental and Interstate would be rebranded as Hostess Brands.

Wonder Bread briefly became a casualty during a 2012 bankruptcy declaration by Hostess Brands. Between November 2012 and the summer of 2013, the product ceased production. Flowers Foods, owner of various bread brands acquired Wonder Bread and returned national distribution by September 2013.

Finally dropped amidst the shuffle was the *Town Talk* label. Buried terminally in Pittsburgh it has remained.

A Memorial For An Increasing Desperate Population
Homeless Memorial Plaques:
Intersection of Fort Pitt Boulevard and Grant Street,
Pittsburgh

Each winter solstice evening, December 21st, a candlelight vigil is held beneath a busy downtown Pittsburgh highway overpass. Visitors congregate in front of a memorial wall affixed with bronze plaques commemorating named individuals who've died while homeless in Allegheny County.

Since 1989, on this first day of winter and the year's longest night, the gathering mourns the increased number of destitute deaths. The remembered are lives who've perished from illness, substance abuse, violence and chronic desperation on inhospitable and frigid streets.

Each year the fatalities and bronze plaques augment. The frustration behind finding a long-term solution worsens with the widening gap between wealth and poverty.

Shuffling Assets and Finances Within A Deck of Fraud
Former Clark Candy Bar Production Facility:
503 Martindale Street, Pittsburgh
Former Iron City Brewing Production Center:
3340 Liberty Avenue, Pittsburgh
Former Braun Baking Company Location:
1700 Island Avenue, Pittsburgh

Michael P. Carlow understood the goodwill value of an iconic brand name. In 1991, he established the Pittsburgh Food and Beverage Company promising to resuscitate three deeply financially troubled local institutions with prominent reputations.

The initial pair included the D. L. Clark Company, maker of the *Clark Bar* and the Pittsburgh Brewing Company, producer of *Iron City Beer*. He would add three additional failing regional enterprises to his expanding holdings including the local City Pride Bakery (former Braun Baking Company).

Carlow's initial motives may have appeared designed to return his acquisitions to prominence. The existing corporate headquarters buildings for each were in dismal condition. He had been previously credited with successfully rejuvenating a large cement business and two furniture companies. His reputation clouded objectivity regarding his abilities within the food and beverage industry.

His financial practices with Pittsburgh Food and Beverage were rooted in a series of deceptions, frauds and check kiting. His eventually discovered sleight of hand defrauded one local bank a reported excess of $31 million. His guise of business acumen would be revealed by his October 1994 attempt to purchase Wise Foods. The necessitated examination of his company's financial records unmasked a pattern of shifting and transference of assets.

The collapse of Pittsburgh Food and Beverage Company was swift. Over the subsequent months, he attempted to cover liabilities for certain holdings with unfunded checks from another. Assets disappeared and/or became complicated to trace.

His strategy of anticipating bankruptcy protection that might save him proved ill advised and chaotic. Closer inspection of his company's financial statements merely confirmed his accountability for the accompanying problems.

What became evident during the examination by financial experts was that Carlow was adept at losing money. He lacked the experience and ability to reverse the fortunes for any of his holdings. His acquisition of each fresh entity merely prolonged the charade. He had no personal escape plan. His father Frank was an integral part of the scam.

Upon the public revelation of his culpability, Michael Carlow would plead guilty to embezzlement, conspiracy and tax, wire and bank fraud. In August 1996, he would be sentenced to 8 years in prison and ordered to pay $1.4 million in restitution and back taxes.

His father Frank would be charges with 91 counts for various frauds and obstruction of justice. In 1998, he was sentenced to 87 months in prison. He died two years into his term.

Michael Carlow had learned numerous lessons regarding deception and shifting assets and funds during his Pittsburgh Food and Beverage Company tenure. He did not however, learn how to evade capture or reform his integrity.

While incarcerated during the six years he actually served, he continued attempting to evade the seizure of stolen assets and collection of $6.2 million in additional back taxes due to the Internal Revenue Service (IRS).

In January 2013, he pleaded guilty to obstructing IRS efforts to collect back taxes and penalties. A subsequent judicial ruling added an additional prison sentence of two years and 11 months. Carlow however, was spared having to pay the majority of his IRS debt. A ten-year statute of limitations for their collection had already elapsed.

The status for Carlow's two most high-profile brief acquisitions has remained primary regional.

The Clark Bar was the first American combination candy bar featuring a peanut butter core covered in milk chocolate. The Massachusetts based NECCA confectionary company acquired it following Carlow until their own 2018 bankruptcy. The product is currently produced by the Boyer Candy Company in Altoona, Pennsylvania and distributed regionally.

Pittsburgh Brewing Company continued production of Iron City Beer within Pittsburgh until August 2009. The next production center followed in Latrobe within the same brewery that once produced *Rolling Rock Beer*. Their current and newest homestead features significantly increased production in the former Pittsburgh Glass Works facility in East Deer, Pennsylvania.

IRON CITY BREWERY.

IRON CITY BREWING CO

The Demolition of Tradition and Nostalgia
Former Greater Pittsburgh Drive-In *(Currently Wal-Mart*
Superstore):
299 Lincoln Highway, North Versailles
Renamed: 100 Walmart Drive, North Versailles

The earliest drive-in movie theatres reportedly began in the 1910s. The initial patented drive-in was opened on June 6, 1933 in New Jersey. The concept was to enable theatre patrons, uncomfortable with smaller indoor seating, to view movies within the comfort of their car. Drive-ins appealed to families and especially dating couples for intimacy purposes.

During the 1950s and 60s, drive-in theatres became especially popular with baby boomers. Despite seasonal weather restrictions and the requirement of expansive space, there were approximately 4,000 drive-ins throughout the United States.

Smaller car sizes due to inflated gas prices and the expanding industry of at home video devices doomed the drive-in. Appreciating land values made large land plots attractive to developers to construct malls or multi-building residential and commercial complexes.

Located on Route 30 in the Turtle Creek district, the Greater Pittsburgh Drive-In was opened on May 28, 1954 with a single curved CinemaScope screen. The facility could accommodate 1,000 vehicles and featured a children's playground. A miniature golf course would be added on the hillside adjacent to the box office. Between 1956 and 1986, four additional screens would be added.

Greater Pittsburgh closed at the conclusion of the 1997 season. On March 27, 1998, demolition began on the site. A Super Wal-Mart was constructed and currently operates there.

Nationally, an estimated 300 drive-ins remain in operation. Six states no longer have any. The Pittsburgh metro area still hosts twelve traditional drive-ins that feature new release and classic movies. A lingering sense of nostalgia accompanies the price of admission.

The Permanent Rejection of Mass Shooter George Sodini
Murder Site: LA Fitness
1155 Washington Pike, Bridgeville

George Sodini, 48, had developed an unhealthy obsession towards his repeated rejection by women he sought to date. He observed on a self-created website that he considered himself *not ugly or too weird*. He acknowledged that he hadn't had sexual intercourse in nearly two decades or a sleepover girlfriend in nearly three.

His mania worsened. Peers, family and acquaintances only observed a conventional male pining for love and working as a systems analyst at the law firm of K & L Gates. His frustration continued to mount and early in 2009, he contemplated a shooting spree to generate attention towards himself. He delayed his impulse. He continued to reflect on a permanent solution for his angst.

On July 28, 2009 for unknown reasons, he purchased an inert hand grenade and carried it on a Port Authority bus. A passenger sitting adjacent notified police. Sodini was questioned but not charged.

One week later, life had become unbearable to him. He launched into his previously postponed shooting spree without an exit plan. He'd given up on ever finding his desirable soul mate or sexual princess. He entered unnoticed into a woman's aerobic class at a LA Fitness mall location at approximately 8:15 p.m. He placed a duffel bag on the ground removing two 9mm pistols and a .45-caliber revolver from inside.

He then turned out the lights and began firing indiscriminately. He would kill three women and wound nine other people. He fired a reported 52 shots before turning one of his guns on himself and committing suicide. There was no published indication that he knew any of his victims.

Sodini left many unanswered questions, particularly why his violent outburst was not anticipated by anyone within his circle of contact. Rejection had simply overwhelmed and defined him within his mind. In his will, he left an endowment of $225,000 to the University of Pittsburgh from his estate.

The University would express *no interest* in accepting his gift.

A Disorganized Criminal Enterprise Slandering Pigs
Ronald Melocchi's Business Operation: Back Alley
Vending
610 Monongahela Avenue, Glassport

Organized crime within the Pittsburgh metropolitan area morphed into an odd identity with the 2012 *Operation Pork Chop* gambling scandal. The convicted mastermind and namesake of the ring was Ronald *Porky* Melocchi. He would plead guilty in October 2015 to a felony charge of running a *corrupt* organization and misdemeanor counts for distributing gambling devices and bookmaking.

The case ensnared 16 defendants via wiretaps and enabled state enforcement agents to seize 354 video machines and in excess of a $1 million in cash. The roster of indicted participants included a former mayor, city councilman, police chief, multiple restaurateurs and police officers and even a Frank Sinatra impersonator.

Agreeing to a plea arrangement, Melocchi apologized to the judge for his activities. He acknowledged the embarrassment that tainted his family, particularly his 79 year-old mother. He was sentenced to 10 years probation. None of the participants received jail time. One dozen were given probation and fines.

**A University Voice Professor's Dubious Roommate
Selection
Ricardo Tobia's Murder Site:
511 Kirk Avenue, Pittsburgh**

Ricardo Tobia's musical career peaked with his appearance in the 1976 original Broadway cast of *Pacific Overtures*. He also participated in the subsequent West Coast production. Like many of his performance contemporaries, opportunities thinned afterwards and his career stalled.

His next evolution involved becoming a voice professor at Point Park University. The work remained stable and his tenure lasted 35 years. Some of his students would advance their professional careers crediting his tutelage and support. Tobia became an active local community and Methodist church member frequently augmenting their services with the participation of the Point Park singers.

Tobia maintained a discreet lifestyle residing with a roommate, Joseph Martin, 35, half his age.

Martin had exhibited a troubling pattern of mental illness. In 2016, he reportedly chased Tobia around his house with a sword uttering irrational statements. He was committed to the Western Psychiatric Institute after police discovered swords and knives inside his vehicle.

Despite the potential danger, upon Martin's release, the pair resumed residence together. That decision would result in tragic
consequences.

A relapse of his disturbing behavior erupted two years later. On Tuesday, July 5, 2018, Martin's mother involuntarily committed her son to a psychiatric ward. She indicated to authorities that in a conversation with him the following day, he behaved in a *catatonic, non-lucid, unresponsive manner*. He had confided to her that *demons* had taken over him. The result he feared was that he'd hurt his roommate (Tobia).

His fear proved justified. On Saturday morning, law enforcement investigators discovered Richard Tobia in his bedroom with a fatal bullet wound to the head and a deep slice across his stomach. Tobia's dog Sparky had been fatally shot in the head and cut across the neck. Martin's rampage resulted in excessive blood splattering and smears upon the walls and ceilings of the house. A blood drenched sword and knife were discovered inside.

Following Martin's arrest, his mother indicated that she'd discovered a gun with bullets inside his car. When police retrieved the weapon from her house, they further spotted his bloodied shoes in her basement.

At his September 2000 trial, Martin pleaded guilty but mentally ill for the two killings. He was sentenced to 14-28 years of incarceration with mandatory imposed medical health care. He is currently interned at the State Correctional Institution in Albion.

**The Foul Stench of the Tree of Life Synagogue Attack and Attacker
The Tree of Life Synagogue:
5898 Wilkins Avenue, Pittsburgh**

Robert Gregory Bowers was a loose wire unattached to stability and humanity before he detonated upon a Pittsburgh synagogue.

His parent divorced when he was one and his father died seven years later by suicide while awaiting trial on a rape charge. His mother re-married and relocated to Florida briefly before divorcing following an entire year of marriage. She and her son relocated to Pennsylvania where they lived with her parents in Whitehall due her various health issues.

Bowers grew up detached from social interaction and dropped out of high school before graduation. He began working as a trucker.

The utter disintegration of his character and soul found welcoming influences with neo-Nazi and white supremacist movements. He became a follower of regressive hate and posting explicit and offensive online remarks.

His life at 48 was spinning errantly out of control and his philosophy became more violence oriented and radicalized. On Saturday, October 27, 2018 during Shabbat morning services, he launched an armed attack upon Pittsburgh's The Tree of Life Synagogue.

At 9:45 a.m. three religious services were underway inside where three distinct congregations worshiped. Bowers entered the building with a Colt AR-15 semi-automatic rifle and three pistols. He began firing all four weapons immediately at the scattered 75 people inside the building.

For the next hour, Bowers roamed the premises including the basement seeking potential victims. Police arrived within fifteen minutes with tactical teams following. Officers traded gunfire exchanges with Bowers. Two officers and two SWAT members would be wounded, none fatally, Bowers finally hid in a third floor room where he would crawl out after being shot multiple times.

While being treated for his wounds, he defiantly continued a steady stream of oaths against Jewish people. He stressed that they should die for committing genocide against *his* people.

His shooting rampage ultimately killed eleven people and wounded six, including several Holocaust survivors. The bloodshed was the deadliest attack ever against the Jewish community in the United States.

Bowers was charged by the U.S. Department of Justice with 29 federal crimes. At his appearance in Pittsburgh federal court on October 29, 2018, he was ordered to be held without bail pending his future trial.   Federal prosecutors will be seeking the death penalty.

The trial has yet to be held and in October 2020, it was reported that he was seeking a plea bargain oriented towards evading a death sentence.

He also has 36 state criminal counts pending including *hate crime* charges. Any potential state trial will follow his federal court process. It is unlikely he shall ever know freedom again during his remaining lifetime. Political, religious and numerous constructive oriented organizations denounced his actions globally.

Robert Bowers has since discovered a kinship amongst organizations espousing gender, religious and ethnic hatred. This collection or *his* people remain some of the worlds most polarizing and evil-laced segments of humanity. Their blackened souls remain incapable of tolerance, clear sightedness or even remorse for their sustained ignorance.

#HeartsTogether

**The LaRocca Family's Tentacles and Influence on
Pittsburgh Crime
Chub's Place Restaurant:
810 Ingomar Road, Wexford**

In 1953, Sebastian *Big John* LaRocca evaded deportation proceedings by the Immigration and Naturalization Services based on his criminal record. Several prominent local personalities testified on his behalf during the hearings.

Three years later, he became Pittsburgh's newest dominant family crime boss. He fronted his criminal operations by selling beer equipment and concrete blocks in the Oakland district. He was convicted on several occasions for larceny, receiving stolen property and operating lotteries.

For thirty years, LaRocca reigned above the sewer line. Through bribery and extortion, LaRocca controlled Pittsburgh's politicians, city officials, labor unions and numerous police officers. He expanded operations with other national crime families into Havana, Cuba. When Fidel Castro assumed power, these criminal families were forcibly evicted from the country.

Upon LaRocca's death, Michael Genovese became the crime family's leader. He introduced illegal drug trafficking into their revenue stream. By the late 1980s, the family's influence was declining due to incarceration, aging and reluctance to recruit fresh members.

During that same period, the FBI increased surveillance and investigation into Pittsburgh's leading cocaine traffickers. Arrests, indictments and conviction followed on charges of drug distribution, extortion, murder, robbery, gambling and racketeering. Many of the indicted turned informer and chaos proliferated within the family ranks. By 2008, former leader

Michael Genovese and his successor John Bazzano, Jr. were dead from cancer.

The remaining fragment of the family were headed by Thomas *Sonny* Ciancutti bolstered by high-profile bookmakers John *Duffy* Conley, Jeff Risha, Ronnie *Porky* Melocchi and Robert Iannelli reportedly paying protection monies. The Iannelli family is noteworthy for allegedly conducting their operations out of their Chub's Place restaurant in Wexford.

In 2019, Robert Ianneli and his son were arrested for bookmaking and illegal sports gambling operations. The pair pleaded guilty in September 2020 and was sentenced individually to ten years in prison. Their term would be later modified to probation, no prison time and a $300,000 fine.

On July 8, 2021, the LaRocca Family eulogized a final landmark. Thomas *Sonny* Ciancutti, their last acknowledged leader and Mafia *made man* died at the age of 92.

A Delusional Personality Erupting In Abrupt Violence
Anita *Nicki* Gordon Residence: 788 Elm Spring Road,
Pittsburgh
Beth El Congregation, 1900 Cochran Road, Pittsburgh
India Grocery: 2101 Green Tree Road, Scott Town Center,
Pittsburgh
Ahavath Achim Congregation, 500 Chestnut Street,
Carnegie
Ya Fei Chinese Cuisine, 1980 Park Manor Blvd,
Pittsburgh

Richard Baumhammers began an escalating downward spiral during a 1993 vacation to Eastern Europe. While in the Ukraine, he would later confide to his parents that he'd reportedly achieved a heightened state of euphoria. This happiness would crash by the time he toured Finland. He insisted that he was being followed and harassed.

His paranoia worsened upon returning to Pittsburgh prompting him to commit himself into the Western Psychiatric Hospital. He was diagnosed with delusional disorder and a persecution complex. He moved in with his parents over the next successive years, seeking treatment with eight psychiatrists employing 16 different medications.

His condition hadn't always been pronounced. He'd graduated from Kent State University in 1989 and completed a law degree at the Cumberland Law School in Birmingham, Alabama. He focused on immigration and international law with post-graduate studies at the University of Pacific's McGeorge School of Law.

During the early 1990s, he passed the Georgia Bar exam and lived in Atlanta specializing in International Law. He also began practicing in Allegheny County. He would allow both bar memberships to elapse by 1999.

In 1997, he ceased actively practicing and became involved in a fresh obsession. He moved to Riga, Latvia and rented an apartment a block away from where his grandparents lived during the 1930s. He attempted to file claims with the government to re-capture some of the family's properties lost during the Soviet Union's occupation of Latvia. He was one year too late with his application.

In the fall of 1999, he would be arrested in France for striking a female bartender because he believed that she was Jewish. He was detained for a week at a police station and examined inside a psychiatric ward. Upon his release, he took a flight to Spain and then returned to Pittsburgh.

His internal clock was ticking towards combustion. On April 27, 2000, he purchased a .357 Magnum revolver. The following day, two hours and a 15-mile driving and shooting spree would alter his and several other lives.

At 1:30 p.m. that day, Baumhammers strolled over to the home of his parent's neighbor and friend Anita *Nicki* Gordon. She had lived next door to the Baumhammers for 31 years. He fatally shot her without provocation and then set her house on fire.

Next, he jumped into his black Jeep Cherokee and drove to the Beth El Congregation synagogue in nearby Scott Township. Gordon had been an active member there. He fired into the synagogue windows and spray painted two red swastikas on the building.

Nearby, he approached the India Grocer in the Scott Town Center. He gunned down a shopper and shot the 25-year old store manager in the neck. The wound forced him to become wheelchair bound during the next seven years of his life. He would die at 32 from related complications due to pneumonia.

Baumhammers continued his killing spree into Carnegie where he shot out the plate glass windows of the Ahavath Achim Congregation synagogue. At the Robinson Town Centre, he walked into the Ya Fei Chinese Cuisine restaurant and shot to death both the manager and cook.

His final fatality came when he entered a karate studio in Center. Two men were exercising. Baumhammers pointed his gun at one of the them and then turned and shot the other.

Police were able to pull over his Jeep at 3:30 p.m. in Ambridge. He was charged with 19 crimes including five homicides with special *hate crime* status. A search of his parent's house revealed a manifesto he'd written entitled *Free Market Party*. Titling himself *Chairman*, the text championed the rights of European Americans and ranted against minorities and immigrants. He'd created a website espousing his protest organization consisting of a single member.

On May 1, 2000, Baumhammers was arraigned but the judge ruled he was psychologically unstable to stand trial. That decision stalled the proceedings an entire year. When the trial resumed, a jury then determined after deliberating twenty minutes that he was guilty of all 19 charges. That same jury requested that he be executed by lethal injection.

His death sentence has never been enforced. In 2010, Pennsylvania Governor Ed Rendel signed an execution warrant scheduling his assigned death for March 18, 2010. On February 28th, Allegheny County Judge Jeffrey Manning granted Baumhammers an indefinite stay of execution.

He remains in judicial and legal limbo inside the Greene State Correctional Institute in Franklin. His status awaits rulings on various appeals concerning his sentencing. In November

2019, Baumhammers lost an appeal for both his conviction and death sentence.

MANPASAND

CONGREGATION
AHAVATH ACHIM

A News Personality Floundering Amidst A Career Tumble
KDKA Radio:
Foster Plaza 5, 651 Holiday Drive, Suite 300, Pittsburgh

Traditional AM radio broadcasts have lost significant ground in the battle for listeners, relevance and most significantly, advertising revenues. This dilemma has opened the portals towards anger-oriented commentators ranting over contemporary social issues.

Many of these show hosts are belligerent, misinformed and ethically questionable ranters. Whether their combative assaults are actually truthful or well-researched, a segment of the population has found their confrontational approach entertaining listening. Many of these *performers* are mistaken for credible and reliable experts.

Former WTAE television anchor Wendy Bell has been labeled by numerous sources locally as *uninformed* and *racist*. She was fired in 2016 following such a perceived racist posting on her Facebook account regarding the Wilkinsburg mass shooting. She rebounded with a radio host position at KDKA Radio where she received even worse national attention for an impulsive on-air gaff.

During July 4, 2020, Donald Trump spoke at the Mount Rushmore monument using the opportunity to complain about a coordinated movement to attack and discredit America's forefathers. As with the majority of his theatrical performances, protests and demonstrations accompanied his appearance.

Bell advocated during one of her broadcasts that park rangers should be granted the authority to shoot protesters vandalizing monuments. Her suggestion for excessive enforcement cost her another job when her show was taken off the air.

During the beginning of 2021, she began a new conservative oriented radio position with WJAS. By May, she would be pulled off the air once again based on a *personnel matter* that was reportedly being handled within the company. The personnel matter was never revealed.

Throughout all of her past dismissals, Bell has maintained a social media presence touting her philosophical vision. Her viewer numbers on Facebook have reportedly fluctuated between an extreme peak of 10,000 and declining low of 2,000. A major reason for the numbers dip was that her account was temporarily banned for periods of time for posting videos that spread misinformation on COVID-19 and various other unsubstantiated conspiracy theories.

Bell has nearly a three-decade broadcasting career that has provided her numerous contacts for fresh invention. Being divisive may keep one controversial and in the news, but remaining employed requires sustained viewer numbers. In the cruel media universe, market share stimulates advertising revenues.

In January 2022, a new *Wendy Bell Common Sense* weekend afternoon program debuted on Newsmax Media. Her time slot is historically a dead zone. Once again her past listener following will determine if inflammatory rhetoric stimulates a stable audience or simply consigns her as an extinguishing act.

Excessive Lethal Tasering Over A Suspected Bicycle Theft Police Assault Site:
5100 Block of Harriet Street, Pittsburgh

George Floyd's Minneapolis murder by police in May 2020 has prompted many municipal departments to tighten procedures regarding the detainment and arrest of suspected perpetrators.
During 2021, the Pittsburgh police department suffered a crisis of confidence regarding employing excessive force.

On October 13th, officers were called to a Bloomfield neighborhood to investigate the theft of a bicycle from a porch. There was no clarification whether Jim Rogers, 54, was identified by anyone as the thief. First responding officer Keith Edmonds encountered Rogers who vehemently protested his innocence.

Rogers resisted Edmonds' further questioning and became noncompliant with his subsequent orders. Instead of waiting for back up, Edmonds attempted to subjugate Rogers by tasering him with a stun gun. Rogers continued to resist and Edmonds would continue his assault. He ultimately tasered him a reported nine additional times. The encounter was filmed on a cellphone video by a neighbor. Edmonds and other arriving officers were wearing body cameras.

Rogers was finally forcibly detained on the ground, handcuffed. and lowered into the back seat of a police vehicle. He repeatedly asked for assistance indicating that he couldn't breathe. He requested to be taken to a hospital. He was ignored and sat inside the car for seventeen minutes. His condition appeared to worsen.

It is only speculative that the assembled officers thought Rogers might be exaggerating or mimicking George Floyd's desperate plea before his death. Two officers eventually transported him to UPMC Mercy. En route, Rogers went into cardiac arrest and became unresponsive. The officers inside the vehicle maintained that they presumed he'd merely fallen asleep.

Keith Edmonds knew better. His overreaction now imperiled his own future. He followed the transport vehicle and upon arrival to the hospital, immediately began CPR on Rogers. Doctors took over control from him but too late. Rogers expired at the hospital the following day.

Following an aftermath investigation in March 2022, the city announced that it had terminated five officers involved in the incident without naming them. None would be subjected to criminal prosecution. At that time, a city spokeswoman indicated that Pennsylvania law prohibits the police bureau from releasing publicly officer worn camera footage.

There is a loophole to this prohibition. A family may view the footage in the event they file a lawsuit. On Monday, April 4, 2022, the estate of Jim Rogers filed a federal wrongful death lawsuit against Pittsburgh and eleven named officers.

A Collapsing Infrastructural Component
Fern Hollow Bridge:
Forbes Avenue and South Braddock Avenue, Frick Park, Pittsburgh

On January 28, 2022, hours before President Joe Biden scheduled a local speech, a crumbling component of Pittsburgh's transportation network collapsed. As the snowy commute hour began nearing 6:00 a.m., the Fern Hollow Bridge inside Frick Park buckled.

Biden's speech was organized to promote his $1.2 trillion federal infrastructure plan. The package was signed into law on November 15, 2021. It targeted $550 billion in fresh spending for public transit, passenger rail, bridges, water and sewer systems and numerous bandwidth and Internet related investments.

Ten people were reported injured from the accident and four were admitted to UPMC Presbyterian Hospital. None of the injuries proved fatal despite the potential for a far worse calamity. Several vehicles including a bus were stationary on the bridge at the time of the collapse.

The Fern Hollow Bridge was opened in 1973 and carried traffic over a large ravine in Frick Park connecting the Squirrel Hill and Point Breeze neighborhoods. It replaced an earlier street railway and highway bridge that had been constructed in 1901 and closed during 1972.

The award winning replacement construction was composed of two welded steel girders supported at each end on reinforced concrete caps. The rigid frame support were inclined welded steel legs resting on reinforced concrete thrust blocks. The 446-foot span had last been inspected in September 2021. The span had been rated in *poor* condition since 2011 by the National Bridge Inventory compiled by the

Federal Highway Administration.

Prior to the collapse, the bridge accommodated 14,000 vehicles daily. The collapse was attributed to a weakened west end of the structure. No primary fractures were discovered in the critical areas of the welded steel girders. A replacement bridge is in the process of being designed and built in sections for future installation. The reopened bridge is tentatively scheduled for 2024.

**A Mother and Uber Driver's Brutal Execution
Murder Site:
500 Block Rosecrest Drive and Oak Street, Monroeville**

Christina Spicuzza, 38, was a mother of four working an evening shift as an Uber driver on February 10, 2022. She had spoken with her live-in boyfriend shortly before heading to a client pickup in Pitcairn around 9:00 p.m.

Her passenger turned out to be a lethal nightmare, 22-year-old Calvin Anthony Crew. Dressed in dark clothing with a covered hood, he entered the rear seat of Spicuzza's dark gray Nissan Sentra. Unaware that he was being filmed by a dashcam, he placed his hand on her left shoulder and pointed a 9mm Luger to the back of her head.

Her initial response was *You've got to be joking*. She pleaded with him that she had a family with four kids. He responded callously that he had a family too.

He demanded that she complete her routing near a wooded area in Monroeville two miles away. At 9:34 p.m., he realized that he was being filmed on the dashcam. He reached for the device while continuing to hold the gun to Spicuzza's neck. The footage abruptly terminated.

Parked on level asphalt near the wooded area, Crews fired one shot into her head killing her instantly. He dumped her body 50 feet off the roadway face down. An Amazon delivery driver would discover her corpse the following morning. Crew drove the Sentra back to Pitcairn and abandoned the vehicle.

Immediately following the murder, Crew attempted to access Spicuzza's banking apps on her phone to transfer money to his girlfriend's phone. He left a blatant tracking trail.

Under interrogation, his girlfriend confirmed that she had requested the ride for him using her Uber account. The gun was registered in her name, but she claimed that it had been stolen earlier at a party for one of Crew's family members. She claimed to be unaware of Crew's intentions and not present with him when he entered Spicuzza's vehicle. Police did not charge her with any crimes.

Police investigators required a week to locate the mini-SD card inside the dash camera. The visual account displayed the events preceding the murder in horrid detail.

The brutal and senseless killing culminated Calvin Crew's criminal history dating back to his youth. He was arrested on a separate firearms charge days before a homicide warrant was issued for Spicuzza's murder. He is currently interned and charged with criminal homicide, robbery, tampering with physical evidence and carrying a firearm without a license.

The murder earned him zero financial rewards and left four children cruelly without their mother.

Oak

Author, photographer and visual artist Marques Vickers was born in 1957 in Vallejo, California. He graduated from Azusa Pacific University in Los Angeles and became the Public Relations and Executive Director for the Burbank, California Chamber of Commerce between 1979-84.

Professionally, he has operated travel, apparel, wine, rare book and publishing businesses. His paintings and sculptures have been exhibited in art galleries, private collections and museums in the United States and Europe. He has previously lived in the Burgundy and Languedoc regions of France and currently lives in the South Puget Sound region of Western Washington.

He has written and published over one hundred books spanning a diverse variety of subjects including true crime, international travel, social satire, wine production, architecture, history, fiction, auctions, fine art, poetry and photojournalism.

He has two daughters, Charline and Caroline who reside in Europe.